RECIPES

WILLIAM MORROW

An Imprint of HarperCollinsPublishers

RECIPES

a collection for the modern cook

Susan Spungen

FOREWORD BY MARTHA STEWART

PHOTOGRAPHS BY MARIA ROBLEDO

HarperCollins books may be purchased for educational, business, or sales promotional use. For information please write:

Special Markets Department, HarperCollins Publishers, 10 East 53rd Street, New York, NY 10022.

FIRST EDITION

Photographs by Maria Robledo

Designed by Level, Calistoga, CA

Printed on acid-free paper

Library of Congress Cataloging-in-Publication Data

Spungen, Susan.

Recipes : a collection for the modern cook / Susan Spungen.

p.   cm

Includes index.

ISBN-10: 0-06-073124-9   ISBN-13: 978-0-06-073124-3

1. Cookery.   I. Title.

TX714.S675 2005

641.5—dc22

2005045710

05   06   07   08   09   ❖/TP   10   9   8   7   6   5   4   3   2   1

FOR V. B.

CONTENTS

I JUST FINISHED LOOKING AT EVERY SINGLE PAGE OF THIS WONDERFUL

new cookbook by Susan Spungen. The "collection," as Susan aptly calls this gathering of her favorite, mouthwatering recipes, and the accompanying beautiful photographs are certainly "modern" as Susan says, but they are also "familiar." Familiar in the sense that a silhouette of a designer jacket by Chanel is familiar—you feel that you've seen something like it before, but not quite like what you are looking at now.

I want to cook each and every one of Susan's recipes right now. I was so ravenous when I stopped looking at the pictures that I took the Bucatini with Cherry Tomatoes and Olives recipe from the galleys and put a big pot of water on the stove to boil. Within the time it took the bucatini (my favorite of all pastas) to cook, the topping was made, and I and a friend had a delicious lunch. I next made the Rigatoni with Squash and Caramelized Onions, and although richer and a bit more complicated than the bucatini, it was as if I had been transported to Italy for a spectacular and earthy meal. Next I am going to make the Thai Cole Slaw and, after that, Susan's Tagine-Style Lamb Shanks.

You may be wondering how I know Susan Spungen, and why I want to try all of her recipes. Well, the answers are simple.

Susan came to work part-time at *Martha Stewart Living* when our magazine was just a fledgling periodical. It was my hope and my belief that everyone should learn as much as they could about publishing while working on an immense project like *Living*. She arrived at a photo shoot in East Hampton with her knives ready for the kitchen, expecting to be put to work cooking or baking. Susan's task? She was the ironer, instructed to make sure every wrinkle was ironed away. Susan and I still laugh about the hours she stood at the ironing board, her bare feet aching from standing on rough sisal carpeting, and the nervousness she experienced being entrusted with hundreds of dollars of irreplaceable white bed linens. In retrospect, that well-done job was a great indication that Susan had the wherewithal and stick-to-it-iveness that is the making of a great worker. She worked freelance for a while at *Martha Stewart Living*, taking a full-time job as pastry chef at Coco Pazzo, a trendsetting New York Italian restaurant in the early 1990s. The simple, delicious, and inventive confections she created there in a tiny space in one corner of the bustling kitchen were proof that she had inventiveness, initiative, and a passion for "good things."

When our magazine needed a full-time food editor, Susan was ready for the job, and she rapidly proved herself a fine cook, a very inventive recipe creator, and an excellent food stylist. The combination of artist and cook and stylist and editor—which is what Susan is—is very hard to find, and Susan epitomizes, for me, what a really excellent cookbook creator has to be. When I look at the photographs in this book I see food artfully arranged, beautifully prepared. When I read the recipes I know that the food has to be delicious, and that the recipes will work. When I taste the food,

prepared from the recipes, I know that a passionate person created the recipes—a person who cares about wholesomeness, freshness, quality ingredients, simplicity, flavors, techniques, and careful preparation. I think of her love of food and preparation as "interactive cooking."

Susan's career at Martha Stewart Living Omnimedia was productive and fulfilling for all involved. Her extraordinary department created all the food that graced the pages of our publications and the usefulness and loveliness of the recipes thrilled the readers just as I know these recipes will. Keeping in mind the fact that Susan is both artist and cook, all readers will be delighted at the innate attractiveness of each finished recipe. Results are not "fancy"; rather, they are what we want our food to be each and every day.

Having Susan's book in hand poses a giant problem: what to have for lunch or dinner right now. Luckily, for all of us, we now have more than one hundred recipes to choose from.

WHO IS THE MODERN COOK? I AM THE MODERN COOK, AND SO ARE YOU.

We cook not because we have to, but because we love to. We could go out to a restaurant, order in, or pop something frozen in the microwave, but we often prefer not to. Food and cooking are important parts of our lives, but far from the only things. We like the convenience of a big supermarket, especially a good one, but we also like to shop at our local farmers' markets when we can, seeking out special ingredients and staying in tune with the rhythm of the seasons. We like to try new ingredients and new flavors. We may plant a small herb garden, even if that means just a few pots on the windowsill, since it takes such little effort, saves money, and provides such a boon to our cooking. Our idea of a dinner party includes guests hanging out in the kitchen (doesn't the party always end up there?) for at least part of the time. We don't like wasting time on preparing something that doesn't deliver a satisfying payoff, but we don't mind the time spent on cooking something special. Time is something we never seem to have enough of, so spending it wisely is important.

The recipes in this book are my repertoire; this is my kind of comfort food. It is not cooking that's rich and heavy, although indulgence in moderation is part of the fun. These are the dishes I come back to again and again. I have simplified and streamlined them over time, as I've become more realistic about what can be easily accomplished in the home kitchen. There is nothing particularly faddish here, though there are a few new ingredients or techniques worth knowing about, like the deliciously nutty pumpkin seed oil that I love drizzled over soups and salads, or a side of salmon grilled on a smoky cedar plank over a charcoal fire. Some of my recipes are simple combinations inspired by seasonal ingredients. Some are new twists on the familiar—not just for the sake of twisting, but always to improve or surprise. There are some classic dishes that I have updated for simplicity and ease, making them just right for how we entertain today. I'm not talking about glitzy theme parties, but sharing satisfying food with friends and family. There shouldn't be a great divide between cooking for family and for "company." Guests, whether they are close friends, family, new acquaintances, or business associates, always prefer to be nurtured by a home-cooked meal than to be served some towering restaurant creation that requires explanation and hours of painstaking preparation.

I hope this book will be both inspiring and fun to use. Almost every recipe is accompanied by its own color photograph, making it a wish book for those of you who like to eat with your eyes. The photographs can help you decide which recipes to choose, and give you a clear idea of what the finished dish should look like and how it might be presented. The pictures will encourage you to cook creatively, with an eye to beautiful presentation. I also hope you find the answers to the constantly asked question, "What should I make?"

My simple recipes give clear, complete instructions that will not intimidate novice cooks. There is also plenty here for accomplished cooks who may need new ideas or reminders on basic techniques. Either way, you should feel proud of the food you make, and gather plenty of compliments. There is no greater compliment than being asked for the recipe of a dish you've just served (though plate licking is good, too). I've been asked for many of the recipes in this book as I've been working on it; that's assured me that I'm on the right track. Now I'm thrilled to finally be able share them all with you.

COURAGE IN THE KITCHEN

Cooking should be pleasurable and fun, not just a means to an end and, please, not a scary experience! Confidence is an important quality for the cook. This book will help you develop your courage in the kitchen. These days so many people tell me that they are too intimidated to cook. Others claim that they don't "cook"—they just make salads, or just grill, or just make French toast. I have news for them, that *is* cooking. Be confident in the dishes you have mastered, and use that confidence to attempt some new challenges.

The only way to become confident about doing anything is through practice, and this is especially true when it comes to cooking. Practice cooking. You might as well, since you need to eat every day. You will be surprised to discover that you enjoy cooking as much as you enjoy eating. Cooking is a bit like exercise—you may not always feel like doing it, but you'll always be glad you did, and you'll feel like doing it again.

ON-THE-JOB TRAINING

My culinary career began in 1977 when I worked at a little place in Philadelphia called The Commissary. I took a year off before starting art school, I needed a job, and working with food seemed a natural choice, since I had always loved to cook and bake. The Commissary, still a fond memory for Philadelphians, was a special place. It was staffed by young artists and students who, for the most part, had little professional cooking or restaurant experience. The food that was served there was a revelation to me. I was only seventeen, and although I had cooked from the very exotic and sophisticated *New York Times Cookbook,* I hadn't yet been exposed to the world or traveled very far, only to the U.S. Virgin Islands to visit my grandmother. The Commissary served a crazy quill of food from all over the world in a cafeteria-style setting. Fresh food was brought up all day long from the bustling basement kitchen. There were two soups daily, two "Plats du jour," and green salads tossed to order (what a concept!) with a very mustardy vinaigrette. There was also traditional French charcuterie, and smoked fish that I had to slice and garnish ever so carefully. A few mornings a week, I stood in the demonstration kitchen at the back of the warm wood-and-blue-tile restaurant and make fluffy while-you-wait French omelets in a non-nonstick pan (which often stuck) for customers. Perhaps this is where I learned to keep my cool while cooking even if things weren't going so well. I didn't realize it at the time, but my culinary future was preordained from that point on.

The Commissary was the first of a string of restaurant jobs that I was just working at for money while studying to become an artist. Later, when I gave up on art but still wasn't quite sure what I wanted to do, I continued to work in restaurants and for caterers. Eventually I had so much experience that I could actually apply for cooking jobs and get them. I learned a great deal from coworkers who had gone to cooking school or trained in French restaurants, so I had the advantage of learning good technique and classical cuisine while on the job. This unconventional training and years of learning by doing gave me the confidence to decide for myself which rules to keep, and which to reject. There is no shame in being a self-taught cook!

Fast forward to 1990: I am standing in the dining room of a not-yet-open restaurant called Coco Pazzo and I am interviewing for a position as pastry chef. Pino Luongo, the renowned restaurateur, was opening a new Tuscan (kind of) place on the Upper East Side of Manhattan and it promised to be exciting. I had already had a taste of magazine work, contributing to the first test issues of *Martha Stewart Living,* and wasn't too keen on going back into a restaurant kitchen. I couldn't seem to persuade Coco Pazzo's chef, Mark Strausman, that I wasn't cut out for the job. He was sure I was, so eventually I agreed to take it. Well, Coco Pazzo was exciting, and very popular. Everyone who was anyone was coming in for lunch and dinner and I was creating what I thought Tuscans would eat for dessert if they did eat dessert (which they don't really do). It all worked, and we received three stars from the *New York Times!* Naturally, this bolstered my confidence and confirmed my belief that rules were meant to be broken!

LIFE WITH MARTHA

All of this prepared me for life with Martha Stewart, as the food editor for a brand-new magazine, *Martha Stewart Living.* I was excited by the prospect of something new and creative and full of

possibility, doing what I loved best. It was just a slightly different application of my skills. Instead of turning out the same food night after night, I would have the chance to create recipes, publish them in a magazine reaching thousands of people, and then move on to the next issue. Even better, since I would be in charge of presenting the food visually in photographs for the magazine, I would be doing what I had been itching to do: combine my two passions, art and food.

Over the next twelve years, I learned what it meant to be a food editor. Editor can mean many different things. A fashion editor helps determine what the trends will be for the next season, and attends lots of photo shoots and fashion shows. A copy editor makes sure all of the *I*s are dotted and the *T*s are crossed. In my case, being a food editor at the then-nascent magazine, which was happily and confidently breaking all the rules—at least in the beginning—meant doing everything that had to do with publishing recipes and food pictures. I came with ideas for recipes, developed them, tested them repeatedly to make sure they worked well, cooked them for the photography shoots, wrote them up for publication, and so on. Over the years, as the company grew, so did my job. I was overseeing all of these activities, now executed by a growing staff of talented cooks and stylists, side by side with other talented editors, with Martha at the helm. I had to give a quick and firm "no" to many good ideas simply because there were just too many of them. I began to realize that less really is more and that being a good editor meant being able to see the difference.

QUALITY AND SIMPLICITY

As you can see, I have always learned things the hard way, by doing, without a road map. Now I can share all of that hard-fought-and-won knowledge, to make things easier for you. It's hard to be simple. It takes experience to be able to figure out what to cast overboard, and what to keep. I often draw an analogy between cooking and art. A painter has to learn basic technique (foundation) before distilling her marks into something more abstract. The same is true for cooking. You have to learn the basics to be able to do "simple" well, or it can just be boring. The better your technique, the better your simple preparations will be. And the better your ingredients are, the less you will have to do to the food. An autumn carrot needs only to be roasted with olive oil, salt, and pepper to intensify its natural sweetness. Sometimes I am amazed by people's surprised delight at quality and simplicity. I strive for them always, and so should you.

LEARNING TO PEEL APPLES

I've always been a teacher at heart. It's easy to remember what it was like the first time I attempted something in the kitchen—what completely mystified me, and how I found the answers. Cooking with less-experienced people—whether training someone new in a restaurant or in the magazine's test kitchen, or cooking with friends in summer rentals, or preparing holiday meals with family—always serves to remind me that no point is too basic to review, no technique too simple to teach, even things such as washing lettuce or peeling apples. Something that seems easy to someone like me, who has practiced hands, may seem difficult to someone who hasn't mastered basic skills. I have taken that into account in this book. I've built as many shortcuts into these recipes as I could, avoiding unnecessary steps—and unnecessary dirty dishes, too.

Pay attention to everything you do when you are cooking. How you handle each of your ingredients or tasks is equally important. If you haven't taken the time to "prep" things properly, the final result will not be as good. The way to become fast at these tasks is not only to practice them to find your own techniques and shortcuts, but also to loathe them, so you can become fast and efficient and get them over with as quickly as possible! That is how I learned to peel apples: I was given two cases of Granny Smiths and an hour to prep them. I quickly taught myself to work in assembly-line fashion. That may not occur to you when you only have four apples to peel, but try peeling a case or two. You'll find it much faster to peel them all, then quarter them all, then core them all, then slice them all.

PRESENTATION IS EVERYTHING

Because I love both food and art, I instinctively understand the importance of presenting food beautifully. Presentation is a huge part of cooking, and it can be learned. Don't slack off at the end: Show off your efforts to their best advantage. It takes no more time to present things artfully, in a way that increases the appeal of the food, than not to. Even when I'm on a buffet line at a party, making a plate for myself, I make it look nice, by arranging the various components so that they complement one another. I even arrange my morning bowl of fruit and cereal so that it is pleasing to my eye. Even if it's only for you, considered presentation enhances the whole experience of eating.

If you like to entertain, have plenty of serving vessels on hand. Platters, bowls, and trays of various sizes are essential. These things don't need to be expensive. Plain white ceramic or porcelain is a good way to start. Buy things when you see them to add to your collection. A table laid with food on unmatched but similar dishes looks unified and appealing. Take into consideration the size, shape, and color of a vessel, and how it will relate to the food you are serving in it. If the food doesn't look good in it, don't be afraid to try something else—larger, smaller, deeper, shallower. You will be amazed at how the right bowl or platter brings a dish to life.

Develop a personal style. This applies as much to presenting food as it does to dressing yourself. Have confidence and trust in what you like and what appeals to you. I like mixing old things with new. I look for clean classic shapes whether I'm shopping at Crate and Barrel, an antiques store, or a flea market, and somehow, they all go together. There *is* a common thread: I chose all of them. Having these things around makes entertaining, and serving food every day, so much more fun.

USING THIS BOOK

Whether cooking for yourself, for your family, or entertaining guests, it should be a pleasure. Learning basic technique is an essential step toward getting satisfaction from the act of cooking. The recipes in this book are organized by their primary technique. When the recipes are hybrids of several different methods, that recipe will be found under the most important technique used. For instance, most of the salads are grouped together in the "Chop" chapter, but you will find two recipes for warm salads, Roasted Squash Salad with Goat Cheese, and Roasted Pear Salad in the "Roast" chapter, since the main ingredients are roasted.

I want to raise your awareness of what you are doing when cooking. When you approach your cooking armed with your new found knowledge, you will become more intuitive and confident. I also hope to help you organize yourself a bit better in your kitchen, especially while menu planning and entertaining. Choosing recipes from different chapters will automatically help you in your planning, so you won't have five things colliding on the stove or in the oven at the same time.

This book addresses just one person, you. But your cooking doesn't have to be a solo performance. It's more fun to cook with others. Put on some music, open a bottle of wine and get your friends and family chopping, peeling, husking, stirring, flipping, whatever you can. Hanging out in the kitchen is as enjoyable as sitting down at the table.

It's always great to have a friend next to you when you're cooking. A friend will lend you a hand. A friend will give you advice without judgment. A friend will boost your confidence. A friend is always around when needed. A friend will share secrets with you. Think of this book as your friend in the kitchen.

PREPARE

MAKING LISTS

Whenever I am going to have a party, I always spend a few minutes making lists. This saves me immeasurable time, not to mention stress, later on. The first list I make is the guest list to help me determine what my menu will be. Is anyone a vegetarian or on a special diet? Will there be adults and children, or just adults? And of course, how many people will there be? This will determine whether it will be a buffet or a sit-down meal, and what kind of food to serve.

The next thing I do is to write up a menu so I can see how it looks on paper. Seeing the various courses or parts of the meal helps me to visualize the food and notice redundancies or a missing piece. Am I forgetting anything? Is it well balanced? Now I can pull any recipes from my files or books or even my head, so I can create a shopping list, the most important list of all. If it's a big party, I start a few days ahead of time to get some big tasks, like making tomato sauce or batches of tart or cookie dough, out of the way. Last minute things like ice, flowers, and very perishable salad greens, are on a separate list since I'll have to make at least one more trip to the store before the party.

Next I write out a prep list: a list of the cooking jobs that need to be done. I find it incredibly helpful to have a prep list, by day, to work from. Again, as with the shopping list, I start with the broad strokes, and fill in the finer details as I go along. Anything that can be done ahead of time should be: squeezing lemons for lemonade, making dressings or sauces, shredding cabbage for slaw, etc. Experience has taught me not to bite off more than I can chew. I used to be overly ambitious, and invariably would run out of time to make something I wanted to serve. If you see it all on paper, you will get a more realistic view of what you can accomplish. No one is going to miss the extra hors d'ocuvre as much as they are going to miss you if you're stuck in the kitchen.

Without lists, you'll burn up a lot of time and energy wondering where to start. If you have a list, you can just start anywhere, and cross things off as you go along. I like to put little boxes next to each item, so I can have the satisfaction of checking them off as I accomplish each task.

EQUIPMENT

Listed below are items that you will find helpful in making the recipes in this book. By adding to your batterie de cuisine *little by little, you will have the right tools on hand to make your cooking easier and faster.*

BAKING OR GRATIN DISHES Shallow oval or rectangular porcelain or ceramic baking dishes come in a variety of colors and they can go from oven to table.

BLENDERS, BAR AND IMMERSION A good bar blender with a strong motor is a must-have in any kitchen. It makes smoother purees than a food processor does for soups and sauces. Immersion blenders are easy to use and to clean, as well as inexpensive. They can also be used to puree soups.

BRUSHES, PASTRY AND BASTING I like flat 1-inch-wide brushes for most tasks. Spend a bit more for better quality brushes; the hairs won't fall out as much.

BUTCHER'S TWINE White cotton kitchen twine is good for trussing chickens, tying up bouquets garnis, and, of course, tying up roasts so they hold their shape.

CAST-IRON SKILLETS If you're buying a new one, look for a "preseasoned" skillet, since it takes years to develop a smooth, seasoned surface on a new pan. Iron skillets are naturally nonstick, and are good for searing meat and fish, and even for roasting a chicken. They are also handy when you need to weight something, like the Pan Bagnat on page 45. Place the skillet on top, and weight it further with a few heavy cans.

CITRUS ZESTER This small hand tool has a short stainless steel head with five small cutting holes used to create threadlike strips of citrus skin. Investing in a better quality tool will ensure lasting sharpness.

DUTCH OVEN/BRAISING POT The best ones are made of enameled cast iron, including the lid. A large bottom surface area is helpful for browning foods in fewer batches. Because they have a nonreactive surface, a stew or braise can be cooked ahead of time, stored, and reheated all in the same pan.

HEAVY-DUTY ALUMINUM FOIL Good for using for foods to be cooked on the grill, such as Foil Packet Beets (page 118), or Grilled Stone Fruit (page 235). It is also the best choice for wrapping a springform pan to make it watertight, as in Lemon Curd Cheesecake (page 230).

INDIVIDUAL RAMEKINS OR GRATINS It's nice to have a set of 6 or 8 so you can make individual portions of crisps, bread pudding, or other baked dishes.

INSTANT-READ THERMOMETER An important tool, even for the experienced cook, for knowing when meat or poultry has reached the proper internal temperature.

KNIVES Your most important tools—without good ones, your cooking will be slow and difficult. An 8-inch chef's knife is your everyday, everything knife. After that, a paring knife, 3 or 4 inches long; a sharp serrated bread knife, at least 8 inches long; and a thin, flexible 8- to 10-inch slicing knife for carving ham, turkey, chicken, roast beef, or lamb round out your basic collection. This is the right knife for slicing cakes and anything delicate and crumbly. If you want to add to that basic collection, a 5- to 6-inch boning knife, a vegetable or meat cleaver, and a pair of kitchen shears would all be good additions.

MANDOLINE, JAPANESE This is a simple tool that makes slicing vegetables and cheese into paper-thin shavings a snap. I especially like it for slicing raw fennel bulbs for salads, but it is also good for carrots, celery, apples, mushrooms, potatoes, and hard cheeses. The plastic Japanese versions with either a metal or ceramic blade are reasonably priced and easy to use. Always use the finger guard, as the blade is very sharp.

MICROPLANE GRATER A carpentry tool turned kitchen tool, this rasp is a favorite of many cooks, including me. It turns hard cheeses into incredibly fine, fluffy wisps that just about melt on your tongue. It is also perfect for grating citrus zest, ginger, garlic, and nutmeg.

MINI FOOD PROCESSOR I use a mini food processor far more often than a large one. It is perfect for making small batches of sauces and dressings that would get lost in a large one. It also tends to chop, rather than puree, herbs, making it perfect for sauces like chimichurri (page 102) or pesto, that benefit from a little texture. The mini food processor is also my top choice for grinding nuts.

NONSTICK FRYING PANS The most useful all-purpose size is a medium pan, 10 inches in diameter. If you add a second, get an 8-inch if you're usually cooking for 4 or fewer people, and a 12-inch if you find yourself cooking for 6 or more people. These have sloping sides and are good for all-around sautéing.

OFFSET SPATULAS I like to have one large and one small offset spatula. These are long, flexible, metal spatulas with a bend just beyond the handle which allows you to easily get the blade underneath foods while keeping your fingers out of the way. They are good for smoothing cake batter, icing a cake, running underneath dough while rolling it out, loosening a baked tart from a piece of parchment paper, and turning delicate foods while they are cooking.

PARCHMENT PAPER, which comes on a roll in white and unbleached versions, is handy for lining baking sheets when making cookies, sifting dry ingredients to save washing a bowl, and for cooking to seal in juices and flavor as in Mushrooms Baked in Parchment (page 164).

PASTRY BLENDER This old-fashioned tool has a straight wooden or plastic handle attached to a semi-oval piece of metal that's divided into five sharp blades at the bottom. Look for those with a thumb rest. When cutting cold butter into flour to make pastry, it helps to have a thumb rest for leverage. Avoid pastry blenders with five wires instead of blades; they aren't strong enough to cut through cold butter, and I find that they easily bend out of shape.

ROASTING PANS You should have at least one large, heavy roasting pan, about 16 by 13 inches, for roasting chickens, turkey, and leg of lamb. For smaller tasks such as roasting vegetables, I also use 9- × 11-inch aluminum baking pans or baking sheets.

RUBBER SPATULAS Large and small, curved or flat, you can never have too many.

SAUTÉ PAN I find it useful to have a 12-inch sauté pan, with straight sides, on hand for browning or sautéing jobs that require a large surface area. I usually use one as an auxiliary pan when browning meats for stews and braises to speed up the job.

SILICONE BAKING MATS one brand is Silpat—come in standard sizes to fit baking sheets. The mats have nonstick surfaces and there's no need to wash pans between batches or reline them with parchment paper. They are easy to wash and can be used repeatedly.

SPRINGFORM PAN A 9-inch springform pan will be fine for the cakes in this book, and for most other recipes calling for one. It is a must for cheesecakes and other cakes with delicate sides and tops. The side of the pan is tightened and loosened with a buckle. After removing, the cake can easily be loosened from the bottom, and slid onto a plate.

TART PANS with removable bottoms come in many shapes and sizes. For the recipes in this book, you will need an 8-inch tart pan.

TONGS Like an extension of your hand, metal tongs allow you to turn and toss food with a quick and deft touch.

VEGETABLE BRUSH A stiff vegetable brush with natural or plastic bristles should be kept by the sink for scrubbing potatoes, carrots, beets, etc.

WHISKS A large balloon whisk is ideal for whipping small amounts of egg whites or cream by hand, or whisking large amounts of eggs for omelets. The large "balloon" shape of the whisk takes some of the elbow grease out of whipping lots of air into mixtures.

FRESH HERBS

Fresh herbs are an essential part of modern cooking—they add a fresh, distinctive flavor to so many dishes. A wide variety of herbs are available at supermarkets everywhere, but they aren't always particularly fresh. Take a good look at them before you buy them if they are in plastic containers, and smell them if you can. Consider planting a small herb garden either in pots or in the ground, close to your kitchen, and keep a few pots of your favorites in a windowsill garden in the winter if you live in a cold climate. The difference in flavor between homegrown herbs and store-bought ones is significant.

They're also easy and inexpensive to grow, and many of them are perennial, so they will regenerate themselves each season. It's also a great way to have access to herbs that are hard to find in stores but that are worth discovering, like lemon verbena, Thai basil, chervil, tarragon, and different types of rosemary, sage, and thyme. I love taking a break from cooking for a walk out to my herb garden to gather a few herbs. It gives me a moment to reflect on nature and reconnect with the sensuality of cooking.

BRONZE FENNEL

LAVENDER

CHIVES

OREGANO

FINO BASIL

CHIVE
FLOWER

SAGE

MARJORAM

DILL

LEMON
VERBENA

THYME

1 medium shallot, finely minced (about
    2 tablespoons)

2 tablespoons balsamic or red wine vinegar

1 tablespoon Dijon or grainy mustard

½ teaspoon kosher salt

Freshly ground black pepper

1 tablespoon freshly chopped herbs such
    as tarragon, chives, chervil, or flat-leaf
    parsley, optional

¼ cup plus 2 tablespoons extra virgin
    olive oil

Everyone should know how to make a good vinaigrette for dressing plain green salads. Here is a basic formula, which can be varied to suit your tastes and needs. Replace half of the vinegar with some lemon juice, substitute a different vinegar, or use a different oil, if you prefer. Use any herbs you like, or omit them altogether. If you like garlic, add a slightly bruised clove to the vinaigrette, and let it sit in the dressing until just before tossing the salad. To make a larger amount, keep a three-to-one ratio of oil to acid.

Whisk together the shallot, vinegar, mustard, salt, a pinch of pepper, and herbs, if using, in a small bowl. Continue to whisk, and slowly drizzle in the oil until emulsified. Use immediately or store in an airtight container in the refrigerator for up to 1 week.

> **Save that almost-empty jar of mustard for making vinaigrette. The mustard that clings to the sides of the jar will be the perfect amount for the dressing, and the jar is a handy alternative to a bowl and whisk. Shake up all the ingredients except for the oil, then add the oil and shake again. Leftovers are already packed for storing.**

VINEGAR · I eat a lot of salad and keep a variety of vinegars in my kitchen. The more aged balsamic vinegar is, the sweeter and thicker it will be. While very old and sweet ones can cost $100 or more, I have never purchased one of these, but I do splurge on one for everyday use that costs about $10. It has the right mild edge for salad dressings or drizzling over grilled fish and vegetables. I sometimes combine balsamic vinegar with lemon juice for more acidity in vinaigrettes. I keep red wine vinegar, rice vinegar, and sherry vinegar on hand, too. It's worth spending more to buy special vinegars since they last so long and add so much flavor.

MAKES 4 CUPS

1 loaf (1 pound) country white bread

There is no comparison between breadcrumbs you make yourself and those you buy. You can control the flavor, texture, and freshness. Besides, it's a thrifty way to use leftover bread. The directions below are for a whole loaf, but of course you can make any amount. Sprinkle some breadcrumbs onto a pasta dish at the last minute for a little crunch.

1 | Preheat the oven to 200°F. Position one rack in the middle of the oven and another rack just beneath it. Place a large baking sheet on the lower rack to catch any crumbs.

2 | Slice the bread about ¾ inch thick. Lay the slices on the upper rack in a single layer. Let bake for 1½ hours. Turn off the heat and let the bread cool completely in the oven. You can leave it overnight if you want.

3 | Grate the bread in a food processor using the grating disk: break the bread into small pieces and feed through the tube. Bread can also be grated on a box grater, or smashed in a resealable plastic bag with a mallet. Store in a resealable plastic bag in the freezer.

ROASTED GARLIC

MAKES 2 HEADS

2 heads of garlic

4 teaspoons extra virgin olive oil

Roasted garlic is much mellower—and more digestible—than raw, but it still adds lots of flavor to dishes. It's easy to make and keeps for a week in the fridge. Once the garlic is cooked and meltingly soft, just cut off the very top with a serrated knife, exposing all the cloves, and give the head a good, firm squeeze into a small bowl. Mash lightly with a fork and you have roasted garlic puree.

Preheat the oven to 375°F. Place the garlic on a large sheet of heavy-duty aluminum foil, drizzle with the oil and wrap loosely. Place in the oven for 1 hour. If not using right away, store in an airtight container for 1 week.

ROASTED PEPPERS

MAKES 1

1 large red, yellow, or orange bell pepper

In summer, I try to remember to throw a pepper or two onto the grill when it's lit so that I always have roasted peppers in the fridge ready to use in sandwiches, salads, or a last-minute antipasto. They're even better when they sit in their own juices for a day or two. You can make more than one at a time, of course.

1. Place the pepper on a hot grill, under the broiler, or on the grate of a gas stove with the flame on medium-high. Roast until the skin is charred all around, turning the pepper with a pair of tongs every 3 to 5 minutes. The pepper should be evenly blackened and there should not be any uncooked spots.

2. Transfer the pepper to a bowl and cover tightly with plastic wrap. Let sit (it will steam as it sits) until cool enough to handle, about 30 minutes.

3. Peel off the charred skin and seed the pepper over the bowl to catch any juices. Remove the core. Use immediately or store in an airtight container for several days.

> Although it's tempting, avoid rinsing the pepper under water, since that will wash away a lot of the smoky flavor and juices. It isn't necessary to remove every bit of charred skin—a little will add flavor.

MAKES ABOUT 24 PIECES

12 plum tomatoes

About 2 tablespoons extra virgin olive oil

1 garlic clove

2 or 3 thyme sprigs

2 or 3 oregano sprigs

Coarse sea salt

Any size or type of tomato can be slow-roasted but the timing will vary depending on the size and juiciness of each tomato; just look for shriveled edges and just a bit of wetness in the center to tell you they're done. Enjoy them on their own, or in salads, sandwiches, tarts, and pizzas. Since the juices are reduced, they won't turn a tart or pizza into a soggy puddle. Their concentrated flavor is something altogether different from that of a fresh tomato. They will keep, layered in a jar and covered with oil, for about a week. The rosy oil left behind can be used in vinaigrettes or as a finishing oil to drizzle over grilled fish or shellfish.

1   Preheat the oven to 350°F, and position the rack in the middle of the oven. Line 1 large or 2 smaller baking sheets with parchment paper.

2   Sliver the garlic as thinly as possible. Cut the tomatoes in half. Cut larger ones in quarters. Arrange the tomatoes, cut side up, on the baking sheet, leaving plenty of space in between. Drizzle each tomato with oil and rub with your fingers to coat well. Sprinkle with the garlic, herbs, and salt.

3   Reduce the oven to 300°F and bake for 2 to 2½ hours, until the tomatoes are shriveled and beginning to brown. Let cool, and transfer to an airtight container or jar if not using right away.

MAKES 4

4 large eggs

1 teaspoon kosher salt

While photographing this book, I often served the crew a simple breakfast of hard-cooked eggs, toast, and sliced melon with a few extras like yogurt, peanut butter, and jams. Everyone seemed to relish this healthy start, and also seemed genuinely fascinated by how to cook eggs this way. Keep in mind that the timing given is for four eggs in a small saucepan. Changing the number of eggs will change the cooking time. Use this recipe as a guideline, and make your own adjustments.

1　Place the eggs in a small saucepan. Add the salt and cover them by 1 inch with cold water. Bring the water to a boil over medium-high heat. Boil the eggs for exactly 1 minute, then turn off heat and let sit for 8 minutes.

2　Transfer the eggs to a colander and run cold water over them to stop the cooking. Eggs can be peeled and served immediately, or can be refrigerated in an airtight container with the shells on for up to 3 days.

＞　This is one case where fresher may not be better. The fresher the egg, the harder it will be to peel. If you have eggs with different expiration dates in your refrigerator, use the older ones here.

SALT　I keep three different types of salt in my kitchen. For most cooking, I use coarse and flaky kosher salt, which is free of additives. I use kosher salt in much of my baking, too, including in cookies, crisp topping, and pastry, since I like the play of salty and sweet in desserts. For desserts that don't benefit from pockets of saltiness, such as most cakes, or if you prefer it, use fine sea salt. As a "finishing" salt, I prefer Maldon sea salt from England. It has a wonderful flaky texture, perfect for sprinkling over foods at the last minute as a crunchy, and of course salty, condiment. It can be crumbled between your fingertips, eliminating the need for a grinder, and it's reasonably priced for salt this good. Whether it's Maldon or some other fine, flaky sea salt, like *fleur de sel* from France, keep some on your table for sprinkling on food. Even your scrambled eggs will seem like a luxurious treat.

HOMEMADE CRÈME FRAÎCHE

MAKES 2 CUPS

2 cups heavy cream

2 tablespoons buttermilk

Crème fraîche is similar to sour cream, but it has a nutty, buttery flavor all its own. Unlike sour cream, crème fraîche can be boiled without curdling so it's excellent for finishing sauces. Try a spoonful with fresh berries, or instead of whipped cream or ice cream with any dessert. You can buy crème fraîche in supermarkets but it's quite expensive. And besides, it's kind of a fun experiment to make it yourself. Buy cream that isn't ultrapasteurized; cream from a local dairy that comes in an old-fashioned glass bottle will work better for making this velvet textured cultured cream.

1. Combine the cream and buttermilk in a clean glass jar. Place the uncovered jar in a saucepan of barely simmering water. When the cream is just warm, remove it and cover tightly with plastic wrap or wax paper, using a rubber band to secure the wrap. Put the jar in a warm place, avoiding drafts.

2. Once thickened, after 12 to 24 hours, stir once, re-cover, and place in the refrigerator, where it will thicken even further and keep for about 2 weeks.

MAKES ABOUT 2 CUPS BEANS AND 2 CUPS BROTH

1 pound fresh unshelled cranberry beans (about 1¾ cups shelled)

1 bay leaf

1 garlic clove, unpeeled

½ small onion, unpeeled, cut in half

1 teaspoon kosher salt

Fresh cranberry beans, also known as borlotti beans, are in season in the summer and fall. Both the pods and the beans are creamy white, streaked with magenta. They are meaty and creamy when cooked, and turn a pale purple color. I love them in salads and soups, such as Soupe au Pistou *(page 182) or as a side dish or a crostini topping (page 193).*

1 | Shell the cranberry beans and rinse with cold water. Combine the beans, bay leaf, garlic, onion, and 3 cups cold water in a small saucepan. Bring to a boil and reduce to a simmer. Cook partially covered, stirring occasionally, until tender when pierced with tip of a paring knife and there is no white in the center of the bean when cut in half, 30 to 35 minutes.

2 | Add the salt and remove from the heat. Let the beans cool in their liquid. Discard the bay leaf, garlic, and onion before using. The beans can be stored for several days in the refrigerator.

> Don't add salt to beans until after they've become tender. If salt is added at the beginning, it will toughen the skins.

MAKES ABOUT 2½ CUPS COOKED LENTILS

1 cup French green lentils

4 cups Golden Chicken Stock (page 178)
    or water

1 bay leaf

1 whole shallot or 1 wedge of onion,
    peeled, with root end intact

A few thyme sprigs

1 teaspoon kosher salt

Lentilles de Puy are tiny and dark olive green, mottled with black before they're cooked. Often referred to as French green lentils, they take only about twenty minutes to cook. Their firm texture makes them perfect for salads such as Squash Salad (page 126). They can also be used to garnish a soup, in place of the barley in Chicken Vegetable Soup (page 181). Once cooked, they will keep in the refrigerator for nearly a week.

Bring the lentils, stock, bay leaf, shallot, and thyme to a boil in a small saucepan. Reduce to a simmer and cook until just tender but still firm, about 20 minutes. Remove from the heat. Add the salt, stir, and let sit for 10 minutes. Drain and rinse well. Remove and discard the bay leaf, shallot, and thyme. Keep in an airtight container in the refrigerator for up to 5 days.

> **The lentils should be al dente when removed from the heat; they will continue cooking as they cool.**

MAKES 1 CUP

1 cup raw almonds, pecans, walnuts,
or hazelnuts

Experiment with your oven to make adjustments to the times given below. Toasted nuts always taste better than untoasted nuts, and they are good warm as a last-minute nibble to serve with wine or cocktails. Always taste nuts before cooking with them to make sure they taste fresh, and use them as soon as possible after purchasing them.

1   Preheat the oven to 375°F. Spread the nuts on a large baking sheet and place in the oven. Shake the pan every few minutes so nuts toast evenly and do not burn. Toast about 6 minutes total for almonds, 8 minutes for pecans, and 10 minutes for walnuts or hazelnuts. The nuts should be fragrant and just golden brown. Immediately transfer to a bowl. (This will prevent them from burning on the baking sheet.)

2   If toasting hazelnuts, cover the bowl with a dishtowel. When cool enough to handle, rub by small handfuls between the palms of your hands to remove loose skins. Use toasted nuts as soon as possible, or store for a few days in an airtight container.

MAKES TWO 8-INCH TART SHELLS

2 cups all-purpose flour

½ teaspoon kosher salt

1 teaspoon sugar

1½ sticks (12 tablespoons) cold unsalted
butter, cut into ¼-inch pieces

Ice water

This versatile dough can be handled in three ways for slightly different results. For most recipes, such as the Caramelized Onion and Bacon Tart (page 171) or Roasted Tomato Tart (page 172), use the basic dough. If you're in a hurry, don't have a rolling pin, or are intimidated by rolling out a tart shell, you can press the dough into a tart pan, and then chill the shell thoroughly before proceeding. This produces a perfectly acceptable, if not quite as tender crust as a rolled tart shell. For an extra flaky crust, which I like for Caramel Apple Tart (page 225), the butter pieces are left a bit larger, and the dough is folded into thirds, which creates a more layered, flakier dough.

BASIC ROLLED DOUGH

1 Combine the flour, salt, and sugar in a chilled bowl and whisk to combine. Cut the cold butter into the flour using a pastry blender until the largest butter pieces are about the size of almonds. Using your hands, break down the biggest pieces of butter, rubbing them into the flour between your thumbs and fingers until the largest pieces are the size of large peas. Use a fork to stir as you dribble in 2 tablespoons to ¼ cup ice water, a little at a time. To test whether you've added enough water, squeeze a bit of the mixture in your hand to see if it holds together. Firmly press down on the dough in the bowl, giving it one or two kneads until it holds together in a mass.

2 Divide the dough in half. Place each half onto a piece of plastic wrap, loosely gather up the wrap, and firmly press down into a rough circle about 1 inch thick. Each disk of dough will be just the right size for one 8- to 10-inch tart. Chill until firm, at least 1 hour or overnight. The dough can also be frozen at this point for a month or two. Slip into a resealable plastic bag for freezing.

3   When you need to roll it out, let the dough soften until it is malleable, giving it a few whacks with a rolling pin to help it along. Lightly flour your work surface (see below) and roll the dough from the center out, using firm pressure, until it is about ⅛ inch thick, flipping it over and adding more flour to the work surface and top of dough as needed. Starting from the top edge of the dough, roll the dough onto the rolling pin, and then center and unroll it over the top of a tart pan with a removable bottom (see page 15).

4   Using your knuckles, nudge the dough down into the corners of the tart pan, being careful not to stretch it. Fold it gently over the edges of the pan, and run the rolling pin across the top to trim the edges. The edges of the pan will cut through the dough. Again, use your knuckles to gently press the dough against the side of the pan. Wrap in plastic wrap or slip into a resealable plastic bag and chill until ready to use. At this point, it can be refrigerated for 1 to 2 days, or frozen for a week or two.

5   To blind bake the shell, preheat the oven to 400°F. Prick the chilled tart shell all over with a fork. Line the tart with parchment paper or aluminum foil and fill with uncooked rice, beans, pie weights, or another tart pan of the same size to prevent the shell from rising. Fold the foil in toward the center to expose the edges of the pastry. Bake until the edges are golden brown, about 25 minutes. Remove the parchment paper and weights, and bake for an additional 5 to 10 minutes, until the bottom turns golden brown.

PRESS-IN METHOD

Prepare the Basic Rolled Dough through step 1. Divide the dough in half and place one half in a tart pan with a removable bottom (see page 15). (Wrap the other half and refrigerate or freeze it for later use. Return to room temperature before using.)

Working quickly so you don't warm the dough too much, spread it out evenly in the pan and up the sides, pressing with the flat side of your knuckles. Make sure the sides of the tart shell are about as thick as the bottom. Chill until very firm, at least 1 hour. Then proceed with your recipe.

FLAKY DOUGH

1   Combine the flour, salt, and sugar in a chilled bowl and whisk until combined. Cut the cold butter into the flour using a pastry blender until the butter pieces are between ¼ inch and ½ inch. Rub the largest butter pieces between your thumbs and fingers to break them down a bit more.

2   Use a fork to stir as you dribble in about ¼ cup ice water, a tablespoon at a time. To test whether you've added enough water, squeeze a bit in your hand to see if it holds together. If the dough seems dry add another tablespoon or two of water and stir with the fork until the water is evenly distributed and absorbed. Firmly press down on the dough in the bowl, giving it one or two kneads until it holds together in a rough mass. It will be quite raggedy.

3   Shape the dough into a long rectangle on a piece of plastic wrap. Fold the dough into thirds using the plastic wrap to help lift the dough. Cut into 2 equal pieces, wrap in plastic, and firmly press down on the plastic to compress the dough slightly. Refrigerate until firm, at least 1 hour or overnight. The dough can also be wrapped in plastic and frozen at this point for a month or two. To roll out the dough, follow step 3 for Basic Rolled Dough (page 34).

>   **To create the perfect work surface for rolling out dough, wipe the counter you are going to roll on with a damp paper towel, leaving it damp, but not wet. Immediately sprinkle with flour and wipe off excess to the side with your hand. Just enough flour will stick to the surface to make a lightly floured work area.**

YOUR HANDS ARE YOUR BEST TOOL

Although you can certainly make pastry dough in a food processor, I recommend making it by hand, especially if you haven't had much experience doing so. Once you've learned how to walk, so to speak, you can run, but the best way to understand tender, flaky pastry is to make it by hand. Knowing when the butter pieces are the right size or when enough water has been added is much easier to sense with your hands. In a machine, a few seconds too long on the pulse button, and the dough will be overworked.

The trick to making good pastry is using very cold ingredients. Cold butter is cut into one-quarter-inch cubes. Then cut the cold butter into the flour with a pastry blender or a fork. Once the butter is broken down into even smaller pieces, I use my hands to break down any large remaining pieces of butter, rubbing them into the flour between my thumbs and fingers until the largest pieces are the size of large peas. Don't linger over this part, or touch the dough any more than you have to, or the butter will warm up too much. If the dough does start to feel soft, put the bowl in the refrigerator until it firms up again. There should be tiny pieces of cold butter in the dough; they create flakiness.

Next, add only enough ice water—just a few tablespoons—to hold the dough together. I set the bowl on a damp folded towel to keep it from slipping around, and dribble the water in while tossing the butter-flour mixture with a fork to make sure that it is evenly distributed. It's tempting to add a lot of water at this point so it will come together faster, but be judicious; too much water will toughen the baked crust. Squeeze a little dough in your hand; if it holds together it doesn't need any more water. Knead it once or twice to make sure that the water is well incorporated and the dough is holding together. If it looks too dry and crumbly in the bowl, sprinkle on a teaspoon or two of water and knead again just once or twice.

Place on a sheet of plastic wrap, and gather up the sides, forming a disk about one inch thick. Press down with the heel of your hand, wrap again, and chill until firm, at least one hour. The chilling time will allow the butter to become cold again, the water to absorb into the dough, and the gluten in the dough to relax. Don't rush this process, or the dough will be too elastic when you try to roll it out.

Once you've got the hang of it, you can make it in the food processor, but like me, you might find you enjoy the feeling of making it by hand.

CHOP

I THINK OF SALADS AS WORKS OF ART, EACH ONE AN INDIVIDUAL EXPRESSION OF THE EXACT

moment of the season. Without salads, there would be no contrasts, no harmony to our meals, only melody. I call this chapter "Chop" because, for salads, your knife is your main tool. In this section, there's little or no heat involved in the preparations. But even though heat is not a factor, a marvelous transformation still takes place.

I recently ran into an acquaintance while we were both buying vegetables in New York City's Union Square Greenmarket. She explained to me that she had lost her sense of smell, and that she didn't really cook, she only made salads! In my opinion, she shouldn't sell herself short. Creatively combining fresh ingredients *is* cooking. I think it may be the most inspired and certainly most spontaneous form of cooking. Let the produce be your muse and whisper in your ear. It will tell you what to do with it, if you listen. Look for ingredients that are sparklingly fresh.

It makes sense that someone who has little sense of smell, and subsequently has a dulled palate (poor girl) would still find something to love about salads. There are so many other factors that make salads interesting and delicious. The layering of flavors, colors, textures, and temperatures are all easy to understand here, and can be a basic lesson you extend to all of your cooking once you understand the concepts.

Each ingredient in a salad should be distinct, creating a delicious dissonance of flavor, texture, and temperature, and an explosion of color. Keep the components of your salad stored separately. You can prepare the ingredients for a green bean salad the day before you need it, but leave the blanched green beans in one container, the vinaigrette in another, the herbs in another. Maybe you'll want to top it with some freshly poached or hard-cooked egg, still warm. Combine the components just before serving, and you will have an explosion of flavors and textures, instead of gray and soggy beans whose flavor and color have deteriorated. Unlike a soup or a sauce, you *don't* want the flavors to blend.

As for knives, make sure you have good ones. These are your most basic and most important tools that you need for all of your cooking, not just salad-making. Be brave, and use a big knife—an eight-inch chef's knife is the right size for most of your kitchen tasks. Keep it sharp, too. Buy a small sharpener and a steel, and learn how to use them. Remember, you are more likely to cut yourself with a dull knife than a sharp one. A sharp knife glides easily through the food, and is less likely to slip. Good sharp knives will help make your cooking a pleasure.

Get into the "zen" of salad-making as I do. Set up your cutting board on your counter and work from left to right (or vice-versa if left-handed). Chefs are taught this method, and it makes all the difference. Keep your pile of ingredients to your left, washed and ready to go, and your bowls or containers on the right. Work your way through them. Enjoy the repetition and precision of chopping, cutting, mincing, and slicing. Enjoy the moment. And watch your fingers.

PAN BAGNAT

ENDIVE AND BLOOD ORANGE SALAD

SERVES 4

3 blood or navel oranges

3 Belgian endive, outer leaves removed
and bottoms trimmed

2 tablespoons black olive paste

2 teaspoons balsamic vinegar

2 tablespoons extra virgin olive oil

Coarse sea salt and freshly ground
black pepper

Colorful and tart blood oranges come into the market around Christmas time, and last through the spring, but navel oranges can be used anytime to make this simple salad. Add some thinly sliced red onion if you like.

1. Cut off the ends of each orange with a sharp knife. Place orange cut end down and slice off the peel from top to bottom as close to the flesh as possible, making sure to remove all the white pith. Slice each orange crosswise into five or six ¼-inch rounds. Set aside.

2. Break off the leaves from the endive and transfer to a large bowl. Arrange the orange slices on top of the endive.

3. Whisk together the olive paste and vinegar. Slowly drizzle in the oil while whisking. Season salad with coarse sea salt and pepper to taste, and serve immediately. Drizzle the dressing over the salad.

PAN BAGNAT

SERVES 4

FOR THE VINAIGRETTE

1 large garlic clove, coarsely chopped

1 teaspoon anchovy paste

1 tablespoon capers, rinsed

3 oil-cured olives, pitted

Pinch of freshly ground black pepper

2 tablespoons red wine vinegar

6 tablespoons extra virgin olive oil

FOR THE SANDWICH

1 crusty French baguette

1 or 2 Roasted Peppers (page 23)

About ½ cup cherry tomato halves

1 celery stalk, thinly sliced

¼ small red onion, thinly sliced

1 can (6 ounces) light tuna packed in
olive oil, preferably Italian, drained

½ cup oil-cured black olives, pitted
and torn in half

2 Perfect Hard-Cooked Eggs,
sliced (page 27)

1 tablespoon capers, rinsed

Freshly ground black pepper

8 large basil leaves

This sandwich, whose name means "bathed bread," is the classic street food of Nice, and there are few things better for a summer picnic. Usually, sogginess is not a virtue in a sandwich, but this one depends on it. The Provençal vinaigrette should saturate the bread. The longer the sandwich sits, the better it gets. A crusty baguette that can stand up to the bathing is essential.

1   Make the vinaigrette by combining all ingredients in a mini food processor or blender. Blend well, about 30 seconds, and set aside. (This can be made several days ahead of time and stored in an airtight container in the refrigerator.)

2   Slice the baguette lengthwise, toward the bottom third of the loaf and hollow out the top half. Spoon about two thirds of the vinaigrette on both sides of the baguette. Layer the ingredients on the open baguette starting with the roasted pepper, followed by the tomatoes, celery, onion, tuna, olives, eggs, and then the capers. Drizzle the remaining dressing over the top. Sprinkle with black pepper and top with the basil leaves.

3   Close the baguette and wrap tightly in plastic wrap. Place it under a large cutting board and weigh it down with heavy pots or cans for 1 hour. Slice and serve.

PEANUT NOODLES WITH MANGO

SERVES 8 TO 10 AS A SIDE DISH

FOR THE PEANUT DRESSING

¾ cup smooth natural-style peanut butter

3 tablespoons rice vinegar

¼ cup plus 2 tablespoons low-sodium

    soy sauce

4 tablespoons dark sesame oil

1 heaping tablespoon grated ginger

Scant teaspoon red pepper flakes

¾ teaspoon sugar

FOR THE NOODLE SALAD

Kosher salt

1 pound thick spaghetti

2 cups sugar snap peas, strings

    removed, or snow peas

2 ripe mangos

Juice of 1 lime

2 scallions, thinly sliced

½ cup loosely packed cilantro leaves,

    coarsely chopped

¼ cup roasted peanuts

These noodles are the perfect thing to bring to or serve at a summer party. They can be made hours, even a day, ahead of time and they won't become gummy. Mango, while an unorthodox addition, adds juiciness and bright color. Sugar snap peas provide crunch, but don't add them until serving time. Serve with Grill-Roasted Lemongrass Chicken (page 108), Baby Back Ribs with Coffee BBQ Sauce (page 100), or simple grilled chicken breasts.

1. Make the peanut dressing by combining the peanut butter, vinegar, soy sauce, oil, ginger, red pepper flakes, sugar, and ½ cup hot water in a mini food processor. Blend well and set aside. (This can be made several days ahead of time.) Store in an airtight container in the refrigerator.

2. Bring a large pot of water to a boil. Add 1 tablespoon salt and the spaghetti and cook according to package directions, stirring occasionally, until al dente.

3. Meanwhile, bring a small saucepan of water to a boil. Cook the peas until they turn bright green, about 30 seconds. Drain and immediately plunge into a bowl of ice water to stop the cooking. Once the peas have cooled, drain, pat dry, cut in half, and set aside.

4. Stand a mango on the stem end. Using a sharp knife, cut the mango into two large pieces, cutting as close to the large flat pit as possible. Score each half of the mango into 1-inch squares, but don't cut through the skin. Next, run the knife between the flesh and the skin to release the cubes. Place the cubes in a small bowl; repeat with the other mango. Squeeze excess juice from the trimmings into the bowl. Squeeze the lime onto the mango cubes and season with a little salt.

5. When the spaghetti is done, drain, rinse with cold water, and drain again. In a large bowl, toss the spaghetti with the peanut dressing until well coated. Add the peas and three quarters of the scallions and toss to combine. Place the noodles on a large serving platter, sprinkle the mango over the noodles, and garnish with the remaining scallions, the cilantro, and peanuts. Serve immediately. If making in advance reserve about one third of the dressing and toss the noodles with the reserved dressing immediately before serving.

SERVES 4 TO 6

FOR THE JALAPEÑO VINAIGRETTE

4 scallions (dark green tops only),
  thinly sliced

1 to 2 jalapeño peppers, seeds
  removed and chopped

¼ cup loosely packed cilantro leaves

Juice of 1 lime

Large pinch of kosher salt

½ cup olive oil

FOR THE SALAD

1 avocado, peeled and cut into
  bite-size pieces

1 head butter or Boston lettuce

12 cherry tomatoes, halved

Small handful of cilantro leaves

3 ounces ricotta salata

4 scallions (white parts only),
  thinly sliced

Although this salad is largely Mexican in spirit, with its zingy jalapeño dressing, the ricotta salata adds an Italian touch. It is a dense, firm, pure white cheese—a bit salty, unlike Mexican queso fresco, which can be bland. Fresh or aged goat cheese or even feta would be good choices, too.

1 Make the vinaigrette by combining the scallions, some of the jalapeño pepper, cilantro, lime juice, and salt in a mini food processor or blender. Blend or pulse to combine. Continue to process while drizzling in the oil. Once the vinaigrette is well blended, taste and adjust to the desired heat, being careful not to add too much jalapeño at one time.

2 In a small bowl, mix the avocado with about half of the Jalapeño Vinaigrette and set aside. This will prevent the avocado from browning.

3 Assemble the salad by arranging the lettuce leaves in the bottom of a large salad bowl. Add the tomatoes followed by the cilantro leaves. Crumble the cheese over the top and sprinkle with the scallions. Place the avocado in the center. Drizzle the remaining dressing on the salad or serve on the side.

> Buy firm avocadoes a few days before you need them and let them ripen on the counter, since it's hard to find ripe ones at the store. If they are ripe, chances are good they've been squeezed a lot, and will have brown spots when cut open.

MAKES 3 QUARTS

2 to 3 large tomatoes (about 3 pounds),
    plus 1 for garnish

2 large red or orange peppers,
    plus 1 for garnish

½ sweet onion, plus ¼ for garnish

2 small or 1 large cucumbers,
    plus 3 small for garnish

⅓ small jalapeño, seeded, plus more to taste

1 garlic clove

2 tablespoons olive oil

2 tablespoons red wine vinegar,
    plus more to taste

Juice of 1 lime

¼ cup loosely packed cilantro leaves,
    plus more for garnish

Kosher salt and freshly ground black pepper

1 ripe avocado

Gazpacho is best in summer, when farm stands and markets are abundant with the necessary ingredients. I always keep a big bowl of gazpacho in the fridge in the late summer: It makes for a great last minute meal for unexpected guests, and the chunky soup only gets better as it sits.

1 | Cut the tomatoes in half and gently squeeze out seeds. Coarsely chop the tomatoes, peppers, onion, cucumbers, jalapeño, and garlic, and toss them together in a big bowl. Working in batches, puree the vegetables in a blender adding ¼ cup water, some oil, vinegar, and lime juice to each batch. Pour each addition into a large bowl. When blending the final batch, puree the vegetables and add ¼ cup cilantro and pulse a few times. Transfer to the bowl and stir well to combine and season to taste with salt and pepper. Cover with plastic wrap and refrigerate overnight.

2 | Just before serving adjust seasoning with salt, black pepper, jalapeño, and vinegar. Cut the remaining tomato, pepper, cucumbers, and the avocado into 1-inch chunks. Finely dice the quarter onion and coarsely chop the cilantro. Add all of the vegetables to the chilled puree and stir well. You could also toss all of the vegetables together and serve on the side, letting each guest garnish their own soup.

OILS

I keep a few cooking oils around my kitchen. Of course, extra virgin olive oil is the one I use most often. I have two: one for everyday uses like dressings and some sautéing, and a more fragrant and flavorful one that I reserve for drizzling on finished dishes, hot and cold, as a condiment. I use pure olive oil, also called light olive oil, when I want a lighter flavor in a dressing, or if I'm sautéing food over very high heat. A "neutral" vegetable oil such as safflower is preferred for delicate dressings and Asian dishes, when I don't want the flavor of olive oil. Dark sesame oil is always good to have on hand for Asian dishes and can also be used as a condiment, but use it sparingly, because too much of it can overwhelm.

THAI COLE SLAW

SERVES 6 TO 8

Juice of 1 orange

Juice of ½ lime

1 tablespoon sugar

2 tablespoons rice vinegar

¼ cup vegetable oil

Pinch of kosher salt

3 tablespoons Thai sweet chili sauce

1 tablespoon Thai garlic chili pepper sauce,
    or to taste

1 pound savoy cabbage (about ½ medium
    head), finely shredded

2 carrots, grated (about ¾ cup)

½ jicama, peeled and cut into thin
    matchsticks

1½ cups mint leaves, coarsely chopped,
    plus whole leaves for garnish

I find it hard to stop eating this cool, minty slaw, often enjoying leftovers right from the bowl while standing in the kitchen. It goes well with Grill-Roasted Lemongrass Chicken or Baby Back Ribs with Coffee BBQ Sauce. It looks better when served within a few hours, but the flavor keeps improving over several days. The two bottled sauces called for are available in the ethnic section of your supermarket; they can also be used to perk up marinades and dressings.

Whisk together the orange juice, lime juice, sugar, vinegar, oil salt, and Thai sweet chili sauce in a small bowl. Add the Thai garlic chili pepper sauce. In a large bowl, combine the cabbage, carrots, jicama, and mint. About half an hour before serving, toss the cabbage with the dressing and chill. Sprinkle with mint leaves for garnish.

THAI CHILI
SAUCES

Made from fresh, hand-picked chiles, and blended with Thai seasonings and some-times garlic. Use it as a condiment or in salads, such as this one. Many supermarkets have well-stocked Thai sections, and you will find it there (see Sources, page 254).

SERVES 4

2 medium fennel bulbs

(about 1 pound trimmed)

1 small crisp red apple

4 celery stalks

Juice of 1 lemon

4 tablespoons extra virgin olive oil

Coarse sea salt and freshly ground

black pepper

About ½ cup freshly grated

Parmigiano-Reggiano

I am crazy about raw fennel, especially when it is sliced paper-thin with a mandoline. Until recently, only expensive, unwieldy mandolines were available in specialty cooking shops, but now there are cheaper and, in my opinion, better Japanese ones available everywhere (see page 14). This salad should be salted at the very last minute so it retains its crispness and volume. (See photograph on the title page.)

1 Trim the fennel so that a few inches of the stalk remains to use as a handle when slicing. Set aside fronds, if any. Quarter the apple, then cut out the core and set aside.

2 Slice the fennel very thin on a mandoline (see page 14) into a large bowl. Slice the celery on an angle on the mandoline, and then the apple, both into the bowl. Pinch off several fennel fronds and add to the bowl.

3 Squeeze the lemon over the salad. Add the oil, then salt and pepper to taste, and toss well. Divide the salad into 4 equal servings and place on plates, stacked high. Sprinkle about 2 tablespoons of the cheese over each salad. Garnish with additional fennel fronds and serve immediately.

> Always rinse your mandoline immediately after using so thin slices of vegetables don't have a chance to dry onto it.

PARMIGIANO-
REGGIANO

This "king" of cheeses is much imitated but never equaled. Similar grana cheeses, so-called for the granularity of the texture, are produced in the United States and elsewhere, but nothing tastes like the real thing from northern Italy. Parmigiano-Reggiano is a cow's milk cheese formed into 75-pound drums that develops a hard, sticky yellow to orange rind as it ages for up to 4 years. Its nutty complex flavor is as good for nibbling as it is for grating over pasta dishes or vegetable soups. Keep the rinds wrapped in plastic in the refrigerator for flavoring soups and stews; be sure to remove the rind before serving. I always have a chunk on hand in the refrigerator. Rewrap it tightly with a fresh piece of plastic wrap every time you use it.

CHOPPED GREEK SALAD

SERVES 6 TO 8

1 large bell pepper, seeded

3 small regular or Kirby cucumbers, seeded

8 ounces feta

2 cups cherry, grape, or other small
    tomatoes, cut in half

½ Vidalia onion, cut into small pieces

1 cup kalamata olives, pitted

¼ cup loosely packed oregano leaves,
    plus more for garnish

1 tablespoon red wine vinegar

Juice of ½ lemon

2 tablespoons extra virgin olive oil

Kosher salt and freshly ground black pepper

Cutting Greek salad ingredients into bite-size pieces makes this a manageable side dish that can be eaten with just a fork and without a struggle at a buffet or picnic. The flavor of fresh oregano is unique, but if you have good dried Greek oregano on hand, you can add some, or even replace all of the fresh with dried. (See photograph on page 106.)

Chop the bell pepper, cucumbers, and feta cheese so that they are approximately the same size as the tomato halves. Transfer to a large bowl and add the tomatoes, onion, olives, and oregano. Drizzle with the vinegar, lemon juice, and oil, and toss well. Season with salt and black pepper to taste. Garnish with oregano leaves and serve.

> **If making this salad an hour or two ahead of time, add the salt just before serving so the salad doesn't become watery.**

CORN SALAD

SERVES 4

4 ears corn (about 2 to 3 cups kernels)

1 Roasted Pepper (page 23)

Juice of ½ lime

1 tablespoon extra virgin olive oil

Coarse sea salt and freshly ground
    black pepper

¼ cup chives cut into ½-inch pieces

For the best flavor, make this simple salad an hour or so before you serve it and don't re-frigerate it. You could also use leftover corn on the cob: Skip the first step and let it come to room temperature for serving. (See photograph on page 65.)

1   Bring a medium saucepan of water to a boil. Cut the kernels off the cobs over a large bowl as directed below. When the water comes to a boil add the corn. Return to a boil and cook for 1 minute. Drain and rinse with cool water and drain well.

2   Transfer to a bowl. Slice the roasted pepper into thin strips and then cut in half lengthwise. Add the roasted pepper, lime juice, oil, and salt and black pepper to the corn and mix well. Garnish with chives.

> When husking corn, leave the stem on if possible so you have something to hold on to when shaving off the corn kernels. Cut off the pointed end of the cob so it stands flat and steady. Choose a large, wide, not-too-deep bowl. Wood is a good choice, since your knife is bound to hit the bowl. A larger bowl will catch the kernels that inevitably go flying, and won't get in the way of your knife. Stand the cob upright in the center of the bowl, gripping the stem, and cut the kernels off using a large sharp knife in a downward motion. Work your way around the cob until all of the kernels are removed. Scrape the cobs with the back of your knife to squeeze as much of the "milk" out as possible.

SAUTÉ

I CALL THIS CHAPTER "SAUTÉ" TO EMPHASIZE QUICKNESS. THINK, "A FLASH IN THE PAN."

Even though the expression refers to bits of gold discovered by the forty-niners, it helps to remember that that's what sautéing is, too. It's cooking food—usually smaller pieces of food—quickly over a high heat and in a relatively small amount of fat. It's in and out of the pan in a flash. The word, which is French, means "to jump." Sautéing often ends up being the method we use when we need something fast, and for just a few people.

Pan-frying (the method used for Potato "Tostones," on page 78) is a close cousin to sautéing, the subtle difference being that pan-frying may use just a bit more fat, and the food may be turned only once, rather than tossed around frequently. Pan-frying has more in common with sautéing than deep-frying, despite the similar names. I never deep-fry at home, mostly because of the mess. I love French fries and fried chicken as the occasional treat out, but I don't cook them at home.

Pan-searing is a variant on sautéing, and usually applies to fish. Striped bass, salmon, or red snapper are all good candidates for pan-searing. To pan-sear something, you start on top of the stove, and finish it in the oven, all in the same pan. The first step is to cook at least one side over a fairly high heat without moving it until it is well browned and crisp. Then it can be cooked over a more moderate heat, either in the oven or on top of the stove, to finish cooking through.

The pan you use for sautéing is important. Technically, a sauté pan is one with straight sides about three inches high. I tend to use what is generally called a fry pan for most of my sautéing, which has sloping slides. I also prefer a nonstick coating, because there's no risk of food sticking to the pan, and it is quick and easy to wash, making a recipe with multiple steps, like the Provençal Layered Omelet (page 62) easy to do. Pans with ovenproof handles can be transferred to the oven when needed, as for Pan-Seared Striped Bass (page 70). A cast-iron skillet can be used here, too. Sloping sides allow you to slide food easily from the pan to a plate, and are a must for omelets. A ten-inch pan can handle most everyday tasks, but it's helpful to have a twelve-inch pan you can press into service when you need to.

Some of the most flavorful and simple pasta dishes are those that start with a few ingredients, quickly sautéed and aggressively seasoned. The cooked pasta is then added to the pan to be tossed with the ingredients and coated with the sauce, which isn't really a "sauce" at all. This gives the pasta a chance to absorb the flavors and for the separate parts to become more integrated into a cohesive whole. The resulting dish is piping hot, full of flavor, and more dressed than sauced.

JUMBO LUMP CRAB CAKES

MAKES 4

1 pound jumbo lump crabmeat

2 teaspoons Dijon mustard

½ teaspoon dry mustard

1 teaspoon Worcestershire sauce

2 tablespoons mayonnaise

1 large egg

Pinch of cayenne pepper

½ to 1 teaspoon Old Bay Seasoning

1 tablespoon chopped flat-leaf parsley

3 slices white bread (such as Arnold
    or Pepperidge Farm), crusts removed

1 tablespoon unsalted butter, for frying

The best crab cake is the simplest one, so the sweet crabmeat can star. Just a few essential and classic flavors—Old Bay Seasoning, Worcestershire, and mustard—is the ideal, with as little bread as possible to hold it all together. Vary the size depending on how you plan to serve them. The recipe below is perfect for dinner, but you could make six smaller cakes for lunch or a first course, or mini crab cakes to go with cocktails. For a quick accompanying sauce, mix together equal parts of Dijon mustard and mayonnaise. Serve with Corn Salad (page 57).

1 | Preheat the oven to 350°F. Place the crabmeat in a large bowl. Gently blot with a paper towel to remove excess moisture, then pick over to remove any bits of cartilage or shell. Shred about half of the crabmeat into small pieces with your hands, toss together with the larger pieces and set the crabmeat aside in the refrigerator.

2 | Combine the Dijon and dry mustards, Worcestershire sauce, mayonnaise, egg, cayenne, Old Bay, and parsley in a small bowl. Whisk to combine. Tear the bread into pea-size pieces, and add to the mixture. Stir to combine and let sit for 5 minutes. Stir again, smooshing the bread with a fork to make a smooth mixture.

3 | Add the bread mixture to the crab and gently fold it in until it is evenly distributed. Divide the crab into 4 equal piles in the bowl. Roll each pile into a ball, then flatten each into a disk about 1 inch thick. Set aside. Chill if not cooking right away.

4 | Heat a 12-inch cast-iron skillet or frying pan with an overproof handle over medium-high heat. Add the butter and sauté the crab cakes until nicely browned, 2 to 3 minutes. Turn them and brown the other side, 2 to 3 minutes. Transfer the pan to the oven and bake for 10 minutes, until heated through.

> Crab cakes can be made in advance and refrigerated for 1 day or frozen for a month. If freezing, wrap each crab cake individually in plastic wrap and then place them in a resealable plastic bag. Thaw them in the refrigerator and blot them with a paper towel to remove excess moisture before sautéing.

SERVES 4 AS A FIRST COURSE, 2 AS A MAIN COURSE

1 tablespoon kosher salt

½ pound bucatini or perciatelli

1 tablespoon extra virgin olive oil

2 garlic cloves, thinly sliced

Large pinch of red pepper flakes

2 heaping cups cherry or grape tomatoes

¼ cup oil-cured or niçoise olives, pitted

1 tablespoon coarsely chopped marjoram

Freshly grated pecorino Romano

I can't resist buying cherry tomatoes (or any type of small tomato) when they're in season, but I never seem to use them all in salads before they start to go soft. Here's a quick and rustic pasta dish that solves the problem. It's particularly fast, since you don't even need to take a knife to the tomatoes; the heat of the pan does all the work. The sauce goes well with bucatini, also called perciatelli, a very thick spaghetti-like pasta with a hole in the middle. Use thick spaghetti if you can't find bucatini.

1 | Bring a large pot of water to a boil. Add 1 tablespoon salt and the pasta. Cook the pasta, using the package directions as a guideline, stirring occasionally, until al dente. During cooking, remove a piece of pasta and taste for doneness.

2 | Heat the oil in a medium frying pan. Add the garlic and sauté until golden brown, about 5 minutes. Add the red pepper flakes and tomatoes and sauté over medium-high heat until the tomatoes begin to break down, about 10 minutes.

3 | Add the olives to the frying pan and continue to sauté over medium heat. As the pasta is finishing, add the marjoram to the tomatoes and reduce the heat to medium.

4 | Drain the pasta, reserving some of the cooking water. Add to the tomatoes and cook for 2 to 3 minutes, adding a few tablespoons of pasta water. Divide the pasta among warmed plates and top with the grated cheese.

WHOLE-WHEAT PENNE WITH SWISS CHARD AND WALNUTS

SERVES 6 AS A FIRST COURSE, OR 4 AS A MAIN COURSE

½ cup walnut halves

Kosher salt

1 pound whole-wheat penne rigati

1 bunch rainbow, green, or red Swiss chard

2 large garlic cloves, thinly sliced

1 tablespoon olive oil

Large pinch of red pepper flakes

1 tablespoon fresh rosemary leaves, coarsely chopped

Freshly ground black pepper

1½ cups ricotta

8 ounces fresh goat cheese

Freshly grated Parmigiano-Reggiano

A colorful bunch of rainbow Swiss chard inspired this recipe. Its stems come in shades of red, white, and golden yellow; the leaves of all are deep green. You can use regular green or red chard, too. Chard is like getting two vegetables in one: the slightly tart, crunchy stems, and the dark green leaves. Since they require different cooking times, they have to be separated by stripping the leaves from the stems with a swipe of your hand.

1 Preheat the oven to 375°F. Spread the walnuts on a large baking sheet and place in the oven. Shake the pan every few minutes so the nuts toast evenly and do not burn, for about 10 minutes. Immediately transfer nuts to a bowl and set aside.

2 Bring a large pot of water to a boil. Add 1 tablespoon salt and the pasta. Cook the pasta, using the package directions as a guideline, stirring occasionally, until al dente. During cooking, remove a piece of pasta and taste for doneness.

3 Wash and dry the chard, and strip the leaves from the stalks. Chop the stalks into ½-inch pieces and set aside. Tear the leaves into medium-size pieces. Set aside.

4 In a large sauté pan, sauté the garlic in the olive oil over medium heat until golden brown, about 3 minutes. Add the red pepper flakes, rosemary, chard stems, and salt and black pepper to taste. Sauté until the stems are tender, about 3 minutes. Add the leaves, cover the pan, and cook until the leaves have wilted, about 5 minutes, stirring once or twice. Remove from the heat and set aside until the pasta is done.

5 Drain the pasta, reserving 1 to 2 cups of the pasta water. Add the ricotta and goat cheese to the chard and stir to combine. Add the pasta and stir until well combined. Season with salt and pepper to taste and add pasta water as needed to moisten the pasta. Transfer to warmed bowls and sprinkle with Parmigiano-Reggiano and walnuts.

Four 6- to 8-ounce striped bass fillets

Coarse sea salt and freshly ground black
　　pepper

Extra virgin olive oil

Aged balsamic vinegar

This basic method that can be used to cook any firm, meaty fish fillet like snapper, grouper, or salmon. Serve with Quickly Stewed Green Beans and Tomatoes (page 72) and a drizzle of syrupy balsamic vinegar over the top. The vinegar doesn't have to be top-of-the-line, eighty-dollars-a-bottle stuff, but it should be a cut above your basic supermarket variety and reserved for use as a condiment (see page 19).

1 | Preheat the oven to 350°F. Rinse the fish and pat dry with paper towels. Transfer to a large plate. Season both sides with salt and pepper and coat lightly with oil.

2 | Heat a large cast-iron skillet or nonstick frying pan over high heat until it is quite hot. If using a cast-iron skillet, coat the bottom lightly with oil. Place the fish skin side up in the pan, reduce the heat to medium-high, and cook until well browned, about 5 minutes. Turn the fillets over with a spatula and cook for 1 minute. Transfer the pan to the oven and cook until the fish is nearly opaque in the center, 7 to 10 minutes. Divide the fish among 4 plates and drizzle with balsamic vinegar.

QUICKLY STEWED GREEN BEANS AND TOMATOES

SERVES 4

1 tablespoon olive oil

3 shallots, cut into ¼-inch rings

Kosher salt and freshly ground black pepper

2 cups cherry, grape, or other small
   tomatoes

1 pound green beans

This quick vegetable dish forms its own sauce, making it a good side dish or bed for a simple grilled or pan-seared fillet of fish, such as Pan-Seared Striped Bass. (See photograph on page 70.)

1 │ Heat a large frying or sauté pan over medium-high heat. Add the oil, shallots, and a pinch each of salt and pepper, and sauté for 7 to 10 minutes. Add the tomatoes, and cook until they begin to split and release their juices, about 3 to 4 minutes.

2 │ Meanwhile, trim the stem end of the beans, leaving the pointy ends intact. Cut them into 2-inch lengths. Gently steam the green beans using a basket-style vegetable steamer until they turn bright green, about 3 minutes. Turn off the heat and uncover, leaving the beans in the pot while the shallots and tomatoes cook.

3 │ Add the green beans, ½ teaspoon salt, and ½ cup water to the frying pan. Cook over high heat for 5 minutes. Serve hot.

RICOTTA MEATBALLS WITH TOMATO SAUCE

RICOTTA MEATBALLS WITH TOMATO SAUCE

MAKES ABOUT 16 LARGE MEATBALLS

1 pound ground veal

1 pound ground pork

3 to 5 slices white bread (such as Arnold or Pepperidge Farm), crusts removed

¼ cup milk

1 cup ricotta

1 large egg, lightly beaten

1 cup freshly grated Parmigiano-Reggiano

2 tablespoons chopped rosemary

2 tablespoons chopped thyme

1½ teaspoons kosher salt

Large pinch of freshly ground black pepper

Vegetable or olive oil, for frying

All-purpose flour, for dredging

Tomato Sauce (recipe follows)

Pellegrino Artusi, author of Science in the Kitchen and the Art of Eating Well, *a classic Italian cookbook, wrote, "Do not think for a moment that I would be so pretentious as to tell you how to make meatballs. This is a dish that everyone knows how to make . . ." Not so today, unless you are Italian-American, and maybe not even if you are. These meatballs can be served on their own or, of course, over pasta. Ricotta cheese lightens their texture, and the combination of pork and veal, rather than beef, lightens their flavor.*

1 | Combine the veal and pork in a large bowl and set aside. Break the bread into pieces and moisten with the milk in a small bowl. Immediately squeeze out any excess milk.

2 | Tear the bread into small pieces over the meat. Add the ricotta, egg, Parmigiano, rosemary, thyme, salt, and pepper. Using your hands, mix well, making sure that the bread is broken up and evenly distributed. Test to see if the mixture is firm enough by rolling some of the meat mixture into a ball about 1½ inches in diameter. Cook one to make sure it holds together and to test the seasoning. If the ball does not hold together and the mixture seems too moist, add 1 to 2 additional pieces of bread torn into very small bits. Repeat the test until the balls maintain their shape.

3 | Form the meat mixture into 1½-inch balls by rolling it with slightly dampened hands. Place the meatballs on a large baking sheet and cover with plastic wrap. Chill until firm. The meatballs can be made a day in advance or frozen at this stage.

4 Heat a large frying pan over high heat and add ¼ inch of oil. You can test to see if the oil is ready by placing a small piece of the meat mixture in to see if it sizzles, or by dipping the handle of a wooden spoon in the oil. When the oil is hot, bubbles will quickly form and rise around the spoon. Dredge the meatballs in the flour, shaking off the excess. Carefully place the meatballs in the pan and fry. (Depending on the size of the pan, this may need to be done in 2 batches.) Turn when golden brown and crisp, after about 5 minutes. As they cook, continue to roll until all sides are crisp, 15 to 20 minutes. Transfer to a platter lined with paper towels to drain briefly. Add to the pot of hot tomato sauce, gently stir, and serve hot.

MAKES ABOUT 2½ CUPS

1 can (28 ounces) whole
   peeled tomatoes in juice

3 tablespoons olive oil

1 celery stalk, finely minced

1 carrot, finely minced

1 medium onion, finely
   minced

2 garlic cloves, minced

2 tablespoons chopped
   flat-leaf parsley

3 tablespoons chopped
   fresh herbs, such as
   oregano, marjoram,
   rosemary, or thyme

Kosher salt and freshly
   ground black pepper

1 tablespoon tomato paste

TOMATO SAUCE

The sweetness of carrots and onions helps balance the acid of the tomatoes in this fast and chunky tomato sauce.

1 Empty the can of tomatoes into a large bowl. Using your hands, remove the cores of the tomatoes. Then break up the tomatoes into small pieces and set aside.

2 Heat the oil over medium heat in a medium saucepan. Sauté the celery, carrot, onion, and garlic until soft, about 15 minutes. Add the herbs, 1 teaspoon salt, and ½ teaspoon pepper, and sauté for 30 seconds.

3 Add the tomato paste and stir until it breaks down, about 1 minute. Add the tomatoes and juice and bring to a boil over high heat. Reduce the heat to a simmer and cook for 10 minutes. Adjust seasoning. Serve immediately with meatballs or store in an airtight container in the refrigerator for several days.

SERVES 6

1½ to 2 pounds small potatoes (about 20)

1 teaspoon kosher salt

Olive oil

Coarse sea salt

These twice-cooked potatoes remind me of plantain tostones that are fried, smashed, and then fried again. Here the potatoes are steamed first, smashed, and then pan-fried until crisp. This is an instance where coarse flaky sea salt is called for, but kosher salt can be used as well.

1 | Fill a large saucepan or stockpot with 1 to 2 inches of water. Place a collapsible vegetable steamer basket in the pan and place the potatoes in the basket. Add the kosher salt, cover, and bring to a boil. Steam over medium heat until the potatoes are just tender when pierced with the tip of a paring knife, about 25 minutes. Be careful not to overcook or they won't hold together when smashed. Drain and set aside until cool enough to handle.

2 | Carefully flatten the potatoes by gently squeezing them, one at a time, between the palms of your hands so that they flatten slightly but remain in one piece; some potatoes will inevitably break but they can still be used. Pour about ¼ inch oil in a medium frying pan and heat over medium-high heat until hot. You can test to see if the oil is ready by placing a piece of potato in to see if it sizzles, or by dipping the handle of a wooden spoon in the oil. When the oil is hot, bubbles will quickly form and rise around the spoon.

3 | Fry the potatoes until they are crisp and brown on the first side, 4 to 6 minutes. Turn the potatoes with tongs and brown the other side, 4 to 6 minutes. Depending on the size of the potatoes and the pan, this may need to be done in 2 or 3 batches. Transfer to a plate lined with paper towels to drain. Arrange on a platter and sprinkle with coarse sea salt. (Keep warm in the oven while frying the rest.)

> To flatten the potatoes, place one in your palm, cover with your other palm as if you were going to clap your hands or make a snowball. Use firm pressure to flatten the potato until the edges crack and it is about half its former thickness. Don't try to flatten the potato completely.

SERVES 4 AS A SIDE DISH OR APPETIZER

½ cup sake or dry white wine

2 tablespoons white or yellow miso

1 tablespoon sugar

1 tablespoon low-sodium soy sauce

Large pinch of red pepper flakes

3 medium to large Japanese eggplant
    (about 1 pound)

2 tablespoons light olive oil or vegetable oil

Kosher salt

Handful of Thai basil, basil, or mint leaves,
    torn if large

Japanese eggplant are pale purple, long, and thin, and have few, if any, of the seeds that can make larger varieties of eggplant bitter. Tiny slender ones, about one to one and a half inches in diameter, can be cut into thick disks. As the eggplant get larger, cut the slices thinner to ensure even cooking. One pound could be anywhere from two to six eggplant!

Look for miso, which is fermented soybean paste, in the dairy section of supermarkets or health food stores. Once opened, it will keep fresh for months in the refrigerator, and can be used in sauces, vinaigrettes, and soups. Serve the eggplant as an appetizer, with toothpicks, or as a side dish with jasmine rice and grilled fish.

1 | Make the glaze: Bring the sake to a boil in a small saucepan. Add the miso and whisk until it is dissolved. Add the sugar, soy sauce, and red pepper flakes. Continue to stir until the sugar is dissolved and the mixture comes to a boil. As soon as it boils, turn off the heat and set aside.

2 | Cut the eggplant into ½- to ¾-inch disks. Heat a large nonstick frying pan over high heat. Add ½ tablespoon of oil and about half the eggplant in a single layer, and sprinkle with salt. Press down gently with a wide spatula and swirl the pan frequently to encourage even browning. Once well browned, 3 to 5 minutes, turn over each piece. Drizzle in another ½ tablespoon of oil, sprinkle with salt, and repeat procedure. The eggplant should be well browned on both sides and soft and creamy on the inside. Transfer to a plate and set aside. Repeat with the rest of the eggplant.

3 | When all the eggplant has been browned, return all of it to the pan. Add the glaze and toss well to combine. Bring to a boil and toss until the eggplant is well coated with the glaze. Add the herbs and toss to combine. Serve immediately.

2 teaspoons olive oil

2 tablespoons plus 2 teaspoons unsalted
    butter

3 shallots, thinly sliced into rings

2 large ears corn, husked and kernels
    removed (see page 57)

Kosher salt

1 cup polenta (cornmeal)

½ cup freshly grated Parmigiano-Reggiano

¼ cup milk

Freshly ground black pepper

Any kind of cornmeal can be used to make polenta. I like to use a medium grind, stone-ground cornmeal if possible. Unless it is specifically labeled "instant polenta" it will take at least fifteen minutes to cook, depending on the coarseness of the cornmeal.

1   Heat the oil and 2 teaspoons of the butter over medium-high heat in a medium frying pan. Add the shallots and sauté until they begin to brown, 3 to 5 minutes, stirring frequently. Add the corn and sauté until brown, 10 to 15 minutes, stirring occasionally. Salt to taste and set aside.

2   In a large, deep saucepan, bring 4½ cups water to a boil. Add 1 teaspoon salt. Slowly sprinkle the polenta into the boiling water, whisking constantly. Once all the polenta has been incorporated, reduce the heat to low, and continue to stir frequently with a wooden spoon. It tends to sputter, so stir with care. Cook about 15 minutes, or until it begins to pull away from the side of the pan. Remove from heat.

3   Add the remaining 2 tablespoons butter, the cheese, milk, and pepper to taste. Stir to combine. Add half of the corn mixture and stir. Adjust salt to taste. Pour into a bowl and garnish with the remaining corn mixture. Serve immediately.

RISOTTO CAKES

MAKES 8 TO 10

About 3 cups leftover Risotto alla Milanese,
cold (page 205)

1 large egg yolk

1 to 2 tablespoons all-purpose flour

½ cup freshly grated Parmigiano-Reggiano

2 to 3 ounces mozzarella or Italian fontina,
cut into ten ½-inch cubes

Cornmeal, for dredging

About 2 tablespoons olive oil, depending
on the size of the pan, for frying

Leftover risotto is just too good to throw away, but it doesn't reheat very well. Add some egg and cheese to the cold risotto, and then shape the mixture into small cakes. Sauté until crisp and serve as a side dish or as a first course with greens.

1 | Preheat oven to 300°F. Combine the risotto, egg yolk, 1 tablespoon of flour, and Parmigiano in a bowl until well combined. Add the other tablespoon of flour if the mixture doesn't hold together. Use a fork to lightly mash some of the rice.

2 | Lightly dampen your hands, and scoop about ⅓ cup of the risotto mixture into one palm. Tuck a small cube of mozzarella in the center, and pat into a burger shape, trying to keep the cheese centered. Dredge in cornmeal and place on a plate until all the cakes are formed. Chill if not using right away.

3 | Heat the oil in a medium frying pan. Cook the risotto cakes, a few at a time, until golden brown, approximately 5 minutes on each side. Drain on paper towels and keep warm on a baking sheet loosely wrapped in foil in the oven until ready to serve. Serve right away, or keep warm for up to an hour.

SERVES 10 TO 12

1 (4 pounds) chicken, cut into 8 pieces

Kosher salt and freshly ground black pepper

2 teaspoons smoked or sweet paprika
(see page 89)

6 to 8 cups fish stock or Golden Chicken
Stock (page 178)

2 teaspoons saffron threads

About ½ cup olive oil

6 links chorizo (about 1 pound),
cut into ½-inch disks

2 ounces sliced Serrano ham,
cut into ½-inch pieces, optional

1 pound head-on shrimp (about 10),
or large prawns

2 small or 1 large yellow onion,
coarsely chopped

4 garlic cloves, finely chopped

1 bunch scallions, thinly sliced, green
and white parts separated

¼ cup chopped flat-leaf parsley,
plus more for garnish

4 cups short-grain Spanish rice

1 can (14 ounces) chopped tomatoes,
or 6 fresh plum tomatoes, peeled
and chopped

1 jar (8 ounces) piquillo peppers,
drained and sliced

½ cup dry white wine, optional

2 dozen littleneck clams, scrubbed

2 dozen mussels, scrubbed

1 cup shelled peas, fresh or frozen

½ pound green beans, trimmed
and cut into 2-inch pieces

Paella is a great party dish; it's easy to make for a crowd, it's a spectacle to behold, and there's something in it for everyone. It is actually easier, as well as more authentic, to cook this dish outside on a kettle grill or freestanding fire pit, than in your kitchen, since the spattering can make a mess of your stove. Otherwise, the technique is pretty much the same, except of course that a grill is hotter and faster. When you cook it on a grill, you get the added bonus of the prized crust, called socorat, of rice left on the bottom of the pan. Have all of the ingredients prepared ahead of time in small bowls or plastic containers (don't put airtight lids on clams or mussels, though, or they'll suffocate) on a couple of trays in the fridge. That way, when it comes time to cook the paella, it will go like clockwork, and there will be hardly anything to clean up.

Spanish rice is as important to paella as Arborio rice is to risotto. Short-grained rice from Calasparra, Spain, is essential for paella. Look for the variety called Bomba, which comes in cloth bags. (See Sources, page 254.)

1 | Wash and dry the chicken. Season with salt and pepper, and then dust with the paprika. Set aside in the refrigerator until you're ready to cook the paella.

2 | Bring the stock to a boil in a medium saucepan and crumble in the saffron. Keep over a low simmer until ready to use. Heat a charcoal or gas grill until medium hot. Coat the bottom of a large (17-inch) paella pan with oil. Add the chicken and cook until golden brown on all sides, turning and rearranging frequently, about 20 minutes. Transfer to a plate and set aside.

3 | Add the chorizo and Serrano ham, if using, to the pan and cook until golden brown, stirring frequently. Transfer to the plate with the chicken and set aside.

4   Add the shrimp and cook until the outsides just begin to brown and the shrimp turn pink, about 2 minutes. Transfer to another plate and set aside.

5   Add the onion, garlic, white parts of scallion, and parsley, and sauté until the onion becomes translucent, stirring frequently, about 5 minutes. Add the rice and cook, stirring frequently, until the rice becomes translucent and just begins to brown, about 10 minutes. Add the tomatoes, piquillo peppers, and wine, if using, letting the rice completely absorb the wine. Pour in 6 cups hot stock and bring to a boil. Cook for 10 minutes.

6   Bury the chicken pieces in the rice. Sprinkle on the chorizo and ham, if using. Arrange the clams and mussels in the rice, seam side up. Cover with the grill cover or heavy-duty foil and cook for 10 minutes more. (If the paella is drying out too soon, add some additional broth or water.) Add the shrimp, peas, and green beans, replace the cover, and cook for 10 minutes more. Garnish with parsley and the green parts of the scallions, and serve immediately.

> To cook paella outdoors, a kettle grill works best, since it is round and the paella pan will fit nicely on it. The lid is useful for the final cooking, when it needs to be covered. You can also use a copper firepit with a low fire made of twigs, not logs, or charcoal so it's easier to control and not too hot. To cover the paella, use a grill cover or foil. To cook the paella inside on the stove, just follow the same directions, and adjust the cooking times if need be. The rice should be al dente but not soupy when finished.

> *Mise en place*, which means "put in place" in French, is a useful concept here. If all of your ingredients are prepared and ready to go, cooking the paella, indoors or out, will be a breeze.

S M O K E D   P A P R I K A

Also known as pimentón, it is an essential seasoning for paella, and is wonderful in many other dishes, including Paprika Roast Chicken (page 132), and almost anything else you might use regular paprika in. The peppers are smoked before they're dried and ground into this haunting spice. It comes in sweet, hot, and bittersweet varieties, but sweet is the most commonly found. Smoked paprika can be easily mail-ordered (see Sources, page 254).

GRILL

WHETHER YOU HAVE A CHARCOAL OR GAS GRILL, LET IT BE THE CENTERPIECE OF YOUR SUMMER

cooking and entertaining. Guests like to watch the food being cooked as much as they like eating it. I'm partial to a kettle grill with a charcoal fire, but I know many people prefer the convenience of a gas grill, and there are many good ones out there these days. It's more fun to grill as a team, so press your significant other, friend, or guest into service for monitoring the grill if you need to be in the kitchen tending to other parts of the meal.

It's almost impossible to give exact timing in recipes for grilled foods. You will have to use your judgment to tell when something is done or needs to be moved to a cooler part of the grill. More than any other cooking method, the variables are the greatest. Cooking times will vary depending on whether you are using lump charcoal or briquets, and charcoal or gas. It will also depend on the weather conditions—is it windy or calm? Is it a hot day, or are you braving cooler temperatures to cook outdoors? Is the food ice-cold or room temperature? All of these factors and many more will cause fluctuating conditions, not just from my grill to yours, but also from one day to the next on your own grill.

Concentrate on getting things nicely seared on the outside, and then move the food to a cooler part of the grill to finish cooking through. The best way to control the heat is to have different areas of the grill at different temperatures. Do this by varying the amount of charcoal in each area before you put the cooking grate on and begin grilling. If you have a gas grill, I still recommend keeping different parts of the grill at different temperatures, and moving the food around accordingly.

One of the advantages of lump, or hardwood, charcoal as opposed to briquets is that you can add some to the fire during the cooking process if the heat starts to fade. Briquets need to ash over before they can be cooked on. Lump charcoal catches very quickly, and bags of lump charcoal have pieces of different sizes, so if you need a quick boost of heat, add a scattering of small pieces of charcoal to your existing fire. The disadvantage of lump charcoal is directly related to its advantages—it burns out more quickly and can be uneven. I often start out with briquets, and add lump charcoal during cooking if I need to make adjustments.

Think of ways to get creative with the grill, using it in many different ways to cook many different things. Grill woks are handy for cooking smaller vegetables, such as asparagus, that would otherwise fall through the grate. Salmon cooked on a cedar plank is a treat that is easy to do and will impress your guests. Chicken cooked over an indirect fire is juicy, slightly smoky, and crisp-skinned. Beets cooked in foil packets on the side of the grill can be used in a salad or as a side dish with meat or fish.

SERVES 6 TO 8

1 loaf rustic bread, cut into thick slices

Several garlic cloves

2 to 3 tomatoes, cut in half horizontally

Olive oil, for drizzling

Coarse sea salt

Spain's version of bruschetta can become a small feast when accompanied by a plate of Serrano ham and manchego cheese. Very ripe, juicy tomatoes are essential for rubbing into the toasted bread.

Heat a charcoal or gas grill to medium hot. Toast the bread on both sides until golden brown. Rub each slice with garlic and then tomato. Drizzle with oil and sprinkle with salt. Serve warm.

Extra virgin olive oil

Ripe heirloom tomatoes

Buffalo or fresh mozzarella sliced
      and at room temperature

Coarse sea salt and freshly ground
      black pepper

Basil leaves, torn if large

Chives, cut into ½-inch lengths

Flat-leaf parsley

There are an astonishing variety of heirloom tomatoes available each summer. They come in so many shapes and sizes, that I cannot give a precise recipe here. Quickly grilling the tomatoes softens them just a bit, and gets their already considerable juices going. The warm tomatoes are topped with cheese, and left on the grill just until the cheese slumps. Serve with the herb salad as a first course or lunch with a crusty loaf of bread to sop up the juicy mess.

1 | Heat a charcoal or gas grill to medium hot and brush the grill with oil.

2 | Trim the tops off smaller tomatoes and cut larger ones into very thick slices, at least 1-inch thick. Place the tomatoes cut side down on the grill until they just begin to warm, 1 to 2 minutes. Turn the tomatoes and top each one with a slice of mozzarella. Cook 1 to 2 minutes more, or until the cheese slumps. Remove the tomatoes from the grill and drizzle with oil and season with salt and pepper. Mix the herbs to make a salad, and scatter generously around the tomatoes. Serve immediately.

MAKES 8 TO 10 SLICES

1 loaf semolina bread

6 to 8 garlic cloves

4 tablespoons unsalted butter, at room
    temperature

2 tablespoons extra virgin olive oil

¼ teaspoon sea salt

Freshly ground black pepper

1 tablespoon chopped fresh rosemary

1 cup freshly grated Parmigiano-Reggiano

Garlic bread was one of the first things I learned to cook as a kid. I like to think I've improved on it here by grilling bread slices, rather than a whole loaf, to maximize the crunchy outsides, and by cooking the garlic to eliminate its raw taste. I prefer using a moist, seeded semolina bread for its sweetness and abundant sesame seeds, but any good bread will work. To prepare in the oven, preheat it to 400°F and toast the bread until the top begins to brown, about eight to ten minutes, reversing the pan from back to front after five minutes.

1 | Heat a charcoal or gas grill to medium low. Cut the bread into 1-inch-thick slices.

2 | Press the garlic into a small saucepan using a garlic press. Add the butter, oil, salt, and pepper to taste and cook over a low heat until the garlic begins to sizzle, 5 to 7 minutes.

3 | Brush both sides of the bread slices with the garlic mixture, picking up some of the garlic each time, and place on a large baking sheet. Sprinkle with the rosemary and cheese. Pat down gently with your hand to help the cheese adhere. Place the bread slices on the grill, cheese side down, and grill until golden brown. Turn and repeat on the other side. The exact time will depend on the heat of your grill. Watch carefully to prevent burning. Keep warm in foil until ready to serve.

BABY BACK RIBS WITH COFFEE BBQ SAUCE

SERVES 4 TO 6

Two 1½-pound racks baby back ribs

Kosher salt and freshly ground black pepper

1 tablespoon olive oil

2 garlic cloves, finely chopped

½ cup espresso or strong brewed coffee

¼ cup red wine vinegar

1 cup ketchup

¾ cup honey

¼ cup low-sodium soy sauce

Cayenne pepper

These ribs can be prepared almost completely ahead of time. They are prebaked and then marinated in the sauce until you are ready to grill them. It just takes a few minutes of grilling to finish them off. The coffee-tinged sauce, which doubles as a marinade, keeps very well for a week or two and can be used as an all-purpose barbecue sauce.

1   Preheat the oven to 275°F. Place the ribs on a baking sheet lined with aluminum foil. Generously season with salt and black pepper. Bake for 2½ hours. Remove from the oven and let cool.

2   Meanwhile, make the BBQ sauce: Heat the oil in a medium saucepan over medium-high heat. Sauté the garlic until it just begins to brown, 3 to 5 minutes. Whisk in the espresso, vinegar, ketchup, honey, soy sauce, a pinch of black pepper, and cayenne to taste. Bring to a boil and reduce to a simmer. Continue to simmer, stirring occasionally, until the marinade thickens, about 30 minutes; the bubbles will get larger and it should coat the back of a spoon. Transfer to a large bowl and set aside. (The marinade can be made up to 2 weeks in advance and stored in an airtight container in the refrigerator.)

3   When the ribs are cool enough to handle place in a resealable plastic bag with the marinade, making sure the ribs are coated evenly on all sides. The ribs can be grilled at this point or left to marinate for up to 2 days in the refrigerator. Turn the bag a few times so they marinate evenly.

4   Heat a charcoal or gas grill to medium low. Place the ribs on the grill. Turn and baste often, about every 5 minutes, watching carefully so they don't burn, until heated through and glazed, about 35 minutes. Cut into individual ribs for serving.

> The ribs can also be finished in the oven. Place on a baking sheet lined with heavy-duty aluminum foil and bake at 450°F for 30 to 35 minutes, basting frequently.

GRILLED SKIRT STEAK WITH CHIMICHURRI

SERVES 6

2 garlic cloves, coarsely chopped

1 shallot, coarsely chopped

½ cup tightly packed flat-leaf parsley leaves

½ cup tightly packed cilantro leaves

½ cup loosely packed oregano leaves

½ teaspoon red pepper flakes

1 teaspoon kosher salt

¼ teaspoon freshly ground black pepper

¼ cup sherry or white wine vinegar

¾ cup extra virgin olive oil

2 pounds skirt steak or flank steak

Chimichurri is as common as ketchup in Argentina. They put it on everything—especially grilled steak of any kind. The sauce keeps well for several days and can be used on any grilled meat or fish.

1 Combine all of the ingredients except for the oil and the steak in a mini food processor. Pulse until finely chopped. Slowly drizzle in the oil and process until all ingredients are well combined, about 30 seconds. (This can be made in advance and stored in an airtight container for several days. To help preserve the color, drizzle a thin layer of olive oil over the surface before sealing the container.)

2 Lightly coat the steak with about half of the chimichurri. Place in a resealable plastic bag and marinate in the refrigerator for at least 1 hour or overnight, turning occasionally.

3 Heat a charcoal or gas grill to very hot. Remove the steak from the marinade, letting any excess drip off. Cook for about 5 minutes on each side, until well browned. Let rest for 5 minutes and slice the meat across the grain on an angle. Transfer to a platter and serve with remaining chimichurri. Serve with Potato "Tostones" (page 78).

SERVES 6

Kosher salt

3 tablespoons light brown sugar

1 teaspoon black peppercorns

1 to 2 rosemary sprigs

Pinch of red pepper flakes

2 bay leaves

6 allspice berries, optional

6 center-cut pork chops, about 1½ inches
    thick (4 to 5 pounds total)

1 tablespoon olive oil, plus more for grill

1 teaspoon balsamic vinegar

1 red onion, cut into thick slices

Freshly ground black pepper

3 ripe but firm peaches, cut in half

Today's pork is bred to be very lean, and less fat means less flavor in the meat. Marinating, or brining, pork chops in a solution of salt, sugar, and herbs and spices renders them juicy and flavorful instead of dry and bland. The salt attracts and retains the moisture in the meat, while the sugar adds flavor and helps the browning. The herbs and spices have time to really permeate the meat, a process that is helped along by the brine. It's well worth thinking ahead to do it.

1   Combine 1 cup water, 3 tablespoons salt, the sugar, peppercorns, rosemary, red pepper flakes, bay leaves, and allspice, if using, in a small saucepan and bring to a boil. Simmer for 5 minutes. Transfer to a large bowl, add 3 cups cold water, and let the brine cool completely.

2   Submerge the pork chops in the brine, cover, and place in the refrigerator for 8 hours or overnight. Before grilling, remove the chops from the brine and pat dry. Discard the brine.

3   Heat a charcoal or gas grill to hot, and brush the grill with oil. Combine 1 tablespoon oil and the vinegar in a small bowl. Skewer each onion slice with 2 perpendicular metal skewers so they do not fall through the grill. Coat with oil and vinegar, and season with salt and black pepper. Add the peaches to the remaining oil and vinegar, season with salt and black pepper, and gently turn them to coat well.

4   Grill the chops 8 to 10 minutes on each side, turning once, until just pink inside or until they reach an internal temperature of 155°F on an instant-read thermometer. Place the onion slices on the grill and cook for about 10 minutes, turning occasionally so both sides cook evenly; they should be juicy, browned on both sides. Grill the peaches cut side down for 1 to 2 minutes, or until nicely browned. Gently turn them with a spatula, and grill the other side until the skins begin to peel away and the juices begin to collect, about 6 minutes, depending on the heat of the grill. Remove the peaches and onion slices from the grill, discarding the peach skins if they fall off, and remove the skewers from the onion. Transfer to a platter with the pork chops and serve immediately.

SERVES 4

½ cup loosely packed flat-leaf parsley
  leaves, plus more for garnish

¼ cup loosely packed rosemary leaves

2 tablespoons olive oil

1 tablespoon dried oregano

2 tablespoons Dijon mustard

1 small shallot, finely minced

Freshly ground black pepper

Top round of lamb (1½ pounds)

Kosher salt

Lamb top round is a great cut for grilling—it cooks evenly and slices easily. It's also a good size for four people, or even two if you want leftovers. The same marinade can be doubled for a butterflied leg of lamb, if you're feeding a large crowd. Serve with Chopped Greek Salad (page 56) and Minted Mashed Potatoes (page 192).

1 | Coarsely chop the parsley and rosemary leaves. Make the marinade by combining the chopped herbs, oil, oregano, mustard, shallot, and pepper to taste in a small bowl. Whisk to combine.

2 | Season the lamb with salt and coat it with the marinade. Marinate in a plastic bag in the refrigerator, covered, for at least 1 hour and up to 2 days.

3 | Heat a charcoal or gas grill to medium hot, and oil the grill. Sear the lamb on each side, about 5 minutes. Move the coals or lower the grill temperature so that the lamb is over indirect heat. Cover and cook for 20 to 30 minutes until an instant-read thermometer inserted into the thickest point reads 140°F, for medium-rare. Let the meat rest for 10 minutes. Sprinkle with fresh parsley, slice, and serve.

SERVES 4

2 stalks lemongrass

1 small shallot, thinly sliced

2 garlic cloves, sliced

2 tablespoons sugar

Heaping ½ teaspoon red pepper flakes

1 teaspoon kosher salt

One 2-inch piece ginger, peeled and
    cut into small chunks

2 tablespoons vegetable oil, plus more
    for coating

2 tablespoons Vietnamese or
    Thai fish sauce (see page 190)

1 tablespoon low-sodium soy sauce

4 baby chickens, about 1 pound each

I particularly like this marinade with tender baby chickens (poussins), *but it also works well with a whole three to four pound chicken, chicken parts, or even boneless breasts. For whole chickens, I use an indirect grilling method, which produces a succulent bird and requires very little attention during cooking. Serve with Thai Cole Slaw (page 53).*

1 Prepare the lemongrass by peeling the two or three outer layers of the stalks. Cut off the fibrous tops about 3 to 4 inches from the bases and set aside. Thinly slice the bottom bulbs.

2 Combine the sliced lemongrass, shallot, garlic, sugar, red pepper flakes, salt, ginger, vegetable oil, fish sauce, and soy sauce in a mini food processor or blender and blend well, about 2 minutes. (The marinade can also be made by mincing and grinding all the ingredients into a paste.)

3 Place the chickens in a resealable plastic bag and pour the marinade over them, making sure they are well coated. Refrigerate for at least 8 hours or overnight, turning once or twice.

4 Set up your grill for indirect grilling: If you have a charcoal grill, light the coals and then push them to one side of the charcoal grate. (Some grills come with two handy metal baskets to hold the coals.) Place a drip pan in the center (optional). Use smoking chips if you like using them. Keep the grill covered except for basting or checking the chickens. If you have a gas grill, preheat the grill with all the burners on high, then adjust the burners on each side of the grill to medium, and turn the burners directly below the chickens off.

5 Remove the chickens from the marinade, letting the excess drip off. Tie the legs of each bird together with the reserved tops of the lemongrass or butcher's twine. Place the chickens in the center of the cooking grate, over the empty space or drip pan. Check the chickens frequently, basting them with the marinade and moving them around the grill as necessary until they are golden brown and the legs of the chickens move easily when wiggled. An instant-read thermometer should register 180°F when inserted into the thickest part of the thighs (1 hour and 15 minutes to 1 hour and 30 minutes). Let the chickens rest for 10 minutes.

SERVES 6 AS A MAIN COURSE, OR MORE

AS PART OF A BUFFET

1 cedar plank

1 side of salmon, skin on (2½ to 3 pounds)

Olive oil

Kosher salt and freshly ground black pepper

1 lemon, cut in half

1 recipe Citrus Relish (recipe follows)

A whole side of salmon is an impressive dish to prepare for a crowd, and grilling it on a cedar plank is much easier than trying to cook it directly on the grill. An untreated cedar plank, widely available at kitchenware shops and hardware stores, is soaked in water to prevent burning. The salmon is arranged on the plank, which is placed directly on the grill. The cedar lends a subtly smoky flavor to whatever is cooked on it, and keeps the food from sticking to the grate. You can use as large a piece of salmon as you want, as long as it fits on the plank. It's okay if it hangs off the sides a bit—the salmon will shrink as it cooks. (See photograph on page 90.)

1   Soak the cedar plank for at least 1 hour and up to 4 hours in cold water. Preheat a charcoal or gas grill until hot, and move the coals to one side of the grill.

2   Lightly coat the salmon with oil and season with salt and pepper. Have it ready in a pan near the grill. Place the soaked plank on the grill until it just begins to smoke, about 1 minute. Turn, using tongs, and repeat on the other side. Once both sides are "toasted," place the salmon skin side down on the plank. Place the lemon halves on the plank next to the salmon.

3   Cover the grill. Check occasionally to make sure the coals are hot enough (if not, add a few) and that the plank is not burning. Move the plank around the grill to maintain the proper temperature. The salmon will take 15 to 20 minutes and is done when the flesh feels fairly firm at the thickest part, and you start to see the fat of the salmon rise to the surface (it will be white).

4   Squeeze the lemon over the fish, and discard. Serve the salmon directly from the plank with Citrus Relish on the side.

>   The key to cooking salmon on a plank is to control the fire; you want enough heat to char the plank and create some smoke to flavor the fish, but not so much that the plank catches fire, taking the fish with it. If this happens, stand by with a spray bottle of water to douse the flames, and move the plank to a cooler part of the grill.

2 navel oranges

Juice of 2 lemons

2 limes, zested and juiced

1 jalapeño pepper, minced

2 tablespoons chopped

    flat-leaf parsley

1 shallot, minced

2 tablespoons olive oil

Kosher salt and freshly

    ground black pepper

CITRUS RELISH

This can be made a day before you want to serve it. Use a zester to remove the colored part of the peel from the fruit in thin strips. A sharp grater with small holes can also be used.

1 Zest the oranges, chop the zest, and set aside. With a sharp knife, cut off the ends of the orange. Place a cut end down and slice off remaining peel from top to bottom as close to the flesh as possible, making sure to remove all the white portion (pith). Holding the orange over a bowl to catch the juice, use a small paring knife to slice in between the membranes. Gently lift out the orange sections. Continue working all the way around the orange.

2 Carefully cut the orange sections into small pieces. Add the orange zest and flesh, lemon juice, lime zest and juice, jalapeño, parsley, shallot, olive oil, and a pinch of salt and pepper to the bowl. Gently stir to combine. Store in an airtight container in the refrigerator.

SERVES 8

1 naval orange

1 tablespoon low-sodium soy sauce

1 tablespoon honey

1 tablespoon grated ginger

Freshly ground black pepper

1 tablespoon rice vinegar

2 tablespoons vegetable oil, plus more
   for grill

Pinch of red pepper flakes

32 large sea scallops, muscle removed
   (see below)

2 cups black rice, cooked according to
   package directions

½ cup cilantro leaves, coarsely chopped

2 scallions (green and light green parts only),
   thinly sliced

Big, juicy sea scallops are one of the fastest and easiest things to grill, and they always seem like a treat. Ask your fishmonger for "dry" scallops, which means they haven't been soaked in a preservative solution. I find skewering them in both directions, creating a grid, is the easiest way to keep them from swiveling around on the grill. Use a large spatula to flip them all at once. Black rice, also called forbidden rice, is fragrant like jasmine or basmati, and a bit chewy like brown rice. It makes a striking backdrop in both color and flavor for the sweet scallops.

1   Soak sixteen 8-inch bamboo skewers in water for at least 1 hour.

2   Zest the orange into a medium bowl; cut the orange in half. Squeeze one half into the bowl and reserve the other half for another use. Whisk in the soy sauce, honey, ginger, black pepper, vinegar, oil, and red pepper flakes. Add the scallops and stir, making sure that they are submerged. Cover and marinate in the refrigerator for at least half an hour, but no more than 1 hour.

3   Heat a charcoal or gas grill until very hot, and oil the grate. Remove the scallops from the marinade, letting the excess drip off. Thread 4 scallops onto each of 4 skewers. Lay them parallel on a large flat plate, and skewer them in the other direction, creating a 4 × 4 grid. Repeat with remaining scallops.

4   Place the scallops on the oiled grate and cook for about 5 minutes on each side, using a wide spatula to turn them all at once, until seared and opaque in the center. Mound the rice on a platter, and remove half or all of the skewers, if desired, and sprinkle with the cilantro and scallions. Serve immediately.

>   **Scallops have a small muscle that attaches them to their shell. It's hard to see, but make sure you remove it, because it will become tough when it's cooked.**

GRILLED ASPARAGUS WITH LEMON BREADCRUMBS

SERVES 6

1 tablespoon plus 1 teaspoon olive oil

½ cup Coarse Breadcrumbs (page 20)

1 lemon, zested and juiced

1 tablespoon chopped flat-leaf parsley
or basil

Kosher salt and freshly ground black pepper

2 bunches asparagus (about 2 pounds),
tough ends snapped off

Although asparagus are now available year-round, I prefer them in the spring when local varieties appear at the farmstands near my Long Island cottage. With their dark purple tops and their fresh, sweet flavor, they have little in common with the out-of-season supermarket variety. I often gild the lily by sprinkling grilled asparagus with crunchy, lemony breadcrumbs to add some textural contrast and a pleasing, tart flavor.

1 | Heat a charcoal or gas grill to medium hot. In a small frying pan, heat 1 tablespoon olive oil. Add the breadcrumbs, lemon zest, half of the lemon juice, parsley, and salt and pepper to taste. Sauté over high heat, stirring frequently, until the breadcrumbs are nicely browned, about 2 minutes. Transfer to a bowl and set aside.

2 | In a bowl, coat the asparagus with the remaining 1 teaspoon olive oil and a pinch of salt. Place the asparagus in a grill basket on the grill, shaking every few minutes. Grill until the asparagus are nicely browned, about 10 minutes.

3 | Transfer the asparagus to a platter. Drizzle the remaining lemon juice over the asparagus and sprinkle the breadcrumbs over the top. Serve immediately.

MAKES 8

2 packages (10 ounces each)
   button mushrooms

½ tablespoon olive oil, plus more for coating

½ tablespoon unsalted butter

Kosher salt and freshly ground black pepper

1 recipe Basic Pizza Dough (page 154),
   made through step 4

Cornmeal, for dusting

8 thin slices prosciutto

About 2⅔ cups shredded radicchio

8 ounces Italian fontina, cut into 8 cubes

Grilled pizzas are popular, but have you ever tried making one? You have to be extremely deft to maneuver them onto the grill and keep them from burning. Calzones—half-moon stuffed pizzas—are much easier to handle. They can be cut into strips to serve as an hors d'oeuvre, or served whole. They can also be made on the stove top in a cast-iron skillet. Just lightly coat the skillet with oil and heat until hot. Cook calzones four to five minutes per side. The fillings below are merely suggestions—you can fill them with whatever you want. Try diced tomatoes, cooked spinach or zucchini, caramelized onions, leftover grilled vegetables, mozzarella cheese, or fresh herbs.

1   Trim and slice the mushrooms. Heat the oil and butter in a large frying pan until hot. Add the mushrooms, a large pinch of salt, and freshly ground black pepper and sauté over high heat, stirring frequently, until the mushrooms are golden brown, about 10 minutes. Set aside.

2   Punch down the risen dough and cut it into 8 equal pieces. Knead each portion into a round. Cover again and let rest 10 minutes. Heat a charcoal or gas grill to medium hot.

3   Dust a clean work surface lightly with cornmeal. With your fingers and palms, flatten one of the dough rounds into a 6 to 8 inch oval about ¼ inch thick. Place a slice of prosciutto over the center of the dough, leaving a 1-inch border all around. On half of the oval arrange about ¼ cup mushrooms, about ⅓ cup radicchio, and 1 cube of cheese.

3   Fold the dough over to enclose the filling. Roll up the edges with your fingers to close tightly and prevent leaking. Lightly brush both sides with olive oil.

4   Place the calzones on the grill and cover. Cook until the dough is firm and golden brown, about 4 minutes. Turn and grill the other side, about 4 minutes. If the outside is done before the inside, move to a cooler part of the grill to finish baking all the way through.

FOIL PACKET BEETS

SERVES 4 TO 6

2 bunches beets (about 8)

1 tablespoon extra virgin olive oil

A few rosemary sprigs

½ teaspoon kosher salt

Freshly ground black pepper

Cooking beets in a foil packet on the grill intensifies their already sweet and earthy flavor. Serve as a side dish with grilled meat or fish, or over greens as a warm salad. Using a stiff vegetable brush to scrub the skins off the beets is much easier than peeling them when they're raw. Scrub until all of the dirt is gone, and you begin to see the color of the beet.

1 | Heat a charcoal or gas grill until medium hot. Trim and scrub the beets. Cut the stems to ¼-inch lengths. Cut the beets so that they are all approximately the same size. If they are small, leave whole.

2 | In a large bowl, toss the beets with the oil, rosemary, and salt and pepper to taste. Tear off an arm's length of heavy-duty aluminum foil. Place the beets in the center of one half of the foil, and add an ice cube. Fold the foil over, and fold the edges over several times until you reach the beets, so you have a rectangular packet. Take care not to tear the foil.

3 | Place the packet on the grill, and, using a spatula, turn over every 15 minutes. Shake the beets around slightly when you do. They will take 30 to 45 minutes total to cook. You can take a peek inside after 30 minutes, toward the end of the cooking time, to see how they're doing. (Just reseal well and return to the grill if they're not done.) They should be tender enough to pierce easily with the tip of a paring knife, and be browned in spots. Open the package, discard the rosemary, and serve warm or at room temperature.

ROAST

IT'S HARD TO GO WRONG WITH ROASTING. A NICE HOT OVEN, AN OPEN PAN, AND OLIVE OIL,

salt, and pepper are just about all you need to create food with a crisp exterior and a moist interior. Just about anything can be roasted with excellent results: meat, fish, vegetables, and even fruit. Generally speaking, roasting happens at temperatures above 375°F but tomatoes are slow-roasted at temperatures as low as 250°F to prevent them from falling apart. Follow a few simple rules, and you will be rewarded with perfectly roasted food every time.

First, you need to have a well-made large, heavy roasting pan that conducts heat well. Sheet pans, baking pans, and cast-iron skillets can be pressed into service if necessary.

Make sure there is plenty of room in your pan. Sixteen by thirteen is a good size. If food is too crowded in the pan, it will steam rather than roast. Two less crowded pans in the oven at the same time are better than one crowded pan, so judge by looking at the ratio of pan surface area to food. Also take into account what the moisture content of the food is when choosing pans. Chicken breasts or peaches need a lot more space than relatively dry potatoes or carrots. The wetter an ingredient, the more space it will need to brown well.

Brown smaller cuts like fish fillets or chicken breasts or beef tenderloin first in a cast-iron skillet or a sauté pan with an ovenproof handle on top of the stove. Then transfer the pan to the oven to finish the cooking. If you don't take this step, the food will be done on the inside before it has a chance to brown on the outside.

Why all this browning? Well, it looks nice; whether it really seals in the juices is a subject of scientific debate, but it certainly seems to. Most important, the brown bits in the pan give you a basis for a flavorful sauce. I use onion slices as a rack when roasting chickens. The onions prevent the birds from sticking, and create flavorful pan juices for deglazing. (Deglazing refers to adding a small amount of liquid—wine or stock—to the degreased drippings to make a pan sauce or gravy.) Make sure that the drippings don't burn. If you notice any burning, just add a little liquid. Once you learn what to look for, you will be whipping up tasty pan sauces like a pro.

To avoid overcooking meat and fish, keep an instant-read thermometer nearby. Don't pierce a chicken or roast repeatedly, or too much of its juices will run out. Allow for "carryover cooking"—the cooking that continues after you've taken something out of the oven. You can always put something back in the oven to cook a little more, but there's no turning back with a chicken that's been overcooked. "Resting" meat or poultry for about ten minutes before slicing it allows the juices to redistrib-

ute within the food. Keep the food warm by tenting loosely with foil during this time.

Roasting vegetables with nothing more than a coating of olive oil and a sprinkling of salt and pepper brings out the vegetables' inherent sweetness. Vegetables are more forgiving than meat; they become sweeter and crisper as they roast. Take them out of the oven when they're as brown as you like them.

Since every chicken, every roasting pan, every oven, and every day is different, learn to trust your instincts when roasting. Use the times given in a recipe as a guideline, paying more attention to the description of how the food should look. If your oven runs hot, either lower the temperature or decrease the time. Most of all, use all of your senses, including common sense, to tell you when something is done.

ROASTED PEAR SALAD WITH GORGONZOLA

SERVES 4

¼ cup hazelnuts or pecan halves

1 bunch arugula

1 bunch frisée or chicory

1 tablespoon coarse Dijon mustard

3 tablespoons balsamic vinegar

Kosher salt and freshly ground black pepper

7½ tablespoons extra virgin olive oil

8 Seckel pears, halved and cored by
    scooping out seeds with a teaspoon

3 shallots, cut into ¼-inch rings

About ½ teaspoon coarse sea salt

About 4 ounces Gorgonzola cheese

4 slices whole-grain Melba Toast
    (recipe follows)

Small Seckels are my preferred pears here, but two ripe Anjou or Bartlett pears can be substituted. Slice the pears into quarters and core. Then cut the pear wedges into three-quarter-inch chunks and proceed as you would with the Seckel pears.

1 Preheat the oven to 375°F. Spread the nuts on a large baking sheet and place in the oven. Shake the pan every few minutes so the nuts toast evenly and do not burn, about 10 minutes total for hazelnuts and 8 minutes for pecans. Immediately transfer the nuts to a bowl and set aside. If using hazelnuts, cover the nuts with a dishtowel. Once the nuts are cool, rub a small handful of nuts between the palms of your hands to remove the loose skins. Continue with the remainder of the nuts.

2 Raise the oven temperature to 425°F. Wash and dry the greens and set aside. Whisk together the mustard, 2 tablespoons of the balsamic vinegar, ½ teaspoon kosher salt, and pepper to taste. Continue to whisk, and slowly drizzle in 6 tablespoons of the oil. Whisk until the dressing is emulsified, then set aside.

3 Slice the pears in quarters if larger than a golf ball. Toss the pears, shallots, and the remaining 1 tablespoon vinegar and 1½ tablespoons oil on a large baking sheet. Season with kosher salt and pepper. Spread the pears out in an even layer with some of the cut sides of the pears down. Transfer to the oven. Shake the pan after 5 minutes and turn the pears using a spatula. Continue to cook 10 to 15 more minutes, shaking the pan and turning the pears frequently until the pears are golden brown all over and just tender. The exact timing will depend on the ripeness of the pears. Remove from the oven and let cool for 5 minutes.

4 Rewhisk the vinaigrette, and lightly dress the greens with the dressing. Divide the greens among 4 plates. Divide the roasted pears and shallots among the 4 plates. Drizzle any remaining dressing over the pears. Crush the nuts lightly using the side of a large knife and sprinkle them over the salads. Season with sea salt and freshly ground pepper. Spread about 1 ounce of Gorgonzola on each piece of toast and place on the side of each plate.

WHOLE-GRAIN MELBA TOAST

Preheat the oven to 350°F. Remove the crusts from thin slices of dense whole-grain bread and slice in half into rectangles. Spread them out on a baking sheet and place in the oven. Toast until the edges are crisp and begin to brown and curl, about 10 minutes. Transfer to a plate. After cooling completely, the Melba toast can be stored for a week or two in an airtight container.

SQUASH SALAD WITH LENTILS AND GOAT CHEESE

SERVES 6 AS A FIRST COURSE, 4 AS A MAIN COURSE

1 medium squash, about 2½ pounds

3 tablespoons extra virgin olive oil, plus more for toasting pepitas

Coarse sea salt and freshly ground black pepper

¼ cup hulled green pumpkin seeds (pepitas)

2½ cups Basic Lentils (page 31)

1 tablespoon balsamic vinegar

2 bunches arugula, washed and dried

4 ounces fresh goat cheese

Pumpkin seed oil, for drizzling

This is a warm salad that can be served for lunch or as part of a buffet. Any firm winter squash such as butternut or kabocha will work here. Nutty green pumpkin seed oil (see below) drizzled over the top gives the salad a distinctive, earthy flavor.

1. Preheat the oven to 450°F. Peel the squash and seed by scooping out the seeds with a spoon or ice cream scoop, and cut into 1-inch chunks. Toss with 2 tablespoons of the olive oil, ½ teaspoon salt, and pepper to taste in a large bowl. Arrange the squash on a baking sheet, leaving plenty of space between the pieces. Roast until the squash begins to brown, about 15 minutes; using tongs, turn each piece over and roast for 15 to 20 minutes more, until the squash is golden brown and very soft.

2. Meanwhile, toast the pumpkin seeds. Lightly coat a small frying pan with oil. When the oil is hot, add the pumpkin seeds and cover the pan with a sieve. (The pumpkin seeds tend to pop and jump out of the pan.) Cook until they puff and brown slightly but still retain some of their green: This will take less than 1 minute. Drain on a paper towel, then transfer to a bowl and toss with salt to taste. Set aside.

3. Dress the lentils by tossing them with the vinegar, the remaining 1 tablespoon oil, ½ teaspoon salt, and pepper to taste. Arrange the arugula leaves on a large serving platter. Arrange the lentils over the arugula and top with the roasted squash. Crumble the cheese over the salad and season with salt and pepper. Sprinkle with the toasted pepitas and lightly drizzle with pumpkin seed oil.

PUMPKIN SEED OIL A very robust, very nutty tasting oil made from roasted pumpkin seeds. It is greenish brown, and has a fantastic aroma and flavor. I love it drizzled sparingly into soups and onto salads as a finishing oil. It should be kept refrigerated to extend its life.

SERVES 4 TO 6

½ cup pecan halves

1 cup Israeli couscous

5 tablespoons unsalted butter, softened

2 shallots, sliced lengthwise

1 celery stalk, thinly sliced

3 tablespoons chopped rosemary,
plus more to season sauce

3 cups Golden Chicken Stock (page 178)
or low-sodium chicken stock

Kosher salt and freshly ground black pepper

About ½ cup dried figs (6 to 8 figs),
cut into quarters

¼ cup dried cranberries

½ cup pomegranate seeds (about 1 medium
pomegranate), optional (see page 131)

½ cup loosely packed flat-leaf parsley,
plus more for garnish

2 small to medium onions, cut into
½-inch slices

2 whole chickens (about 3½ pounds each)

½ cup dry white wine

2 tablespoons all-purpose flour

To me, this is the perfect dish for a Sunday dinner—or any other day. It's homey and comforting, because it's roast chicken, but it's made a bit more special by a fruit and nut stuffing and a rich, dark gravy. I like the crunch of pomegranate seeds in the stuffing, but if that doesn't appeal to you, just leave them out. If you can't find Israeli couscous, which has a wonderful chewy texture, you can substitute cooked barley or wheat berries. You could also use fine-grained couscous, but it won't be as close in texture. Serve with Braised Endive (page 208).

1 Preheat the oven to 375°F. Spread the nuts on a large baking sheet and place in the oven. Shake the pan every few minutes so the nuts toast evenly and do not burn, about 8 minutes total. Immediately transfer the nuts to a bowl and set aside. Raise the oven temperature to 425°F.

2 Toast the couscous in a small saucepan over medium-high heat, stirring occasionally, until golden brown, about 8 minutes. Transfer to a bowl and set aside. In the same pan, melt 1 tablespoon of the butter over medium-high heat. Add the shallots, celery, and 1 tablespoon of the chopped rosemary, and sauté until the shallots begin to turn golden, about 8 minutes.

3 Return the couscous to the pan. Add 1 cup of the stock and season with salt and pepper to taste. Bring to a boil over high heat, then reduce to a simmer. Cover and cook until all the liquid has been absorbed, 8 to 10 minutes. Transfer the couscous to a bowl and cool slightly. Adjust the seasoning and add the figs, cranberries, ¼ cup of the pomegranate seeds, if using, the parsley, and the pecans.

4   In a large roasting pan, arrange the onion slices so they are touching in a single layer at the center of the pan. (The onions will serve as a rack for the chickens and will create a flavorful base for pan gravy.) Wash and dry the chickens thoroughly inside and out. Make sure to rinse out all traces of blood inside the bird. Remove the excess fat around the neck and discard. Season the cavity with salt and pepper. Add the chicken necks, if you have them, to the roasting pan. Stuff each chicken with half of the stuffing. Close the cavity using toothpicks and tie the legs of each chicken together. Rub each chicken with 1 tablespoon of the butter. Season with salt, pepper, and 2 tablespoons of the rosemary. Place the chickens breast side up on top of the onions, facing in opposite directions. Transfer to the oven.

5   After 15 minutes, reduce the oven temperature to 375°F. Roast, basting occasionally with pan juices, until the legs of the chickens move easily when wiggled and an instant-read thermometer registers 180°F when inserted into the thickest part of the thighs (1 hour and 30 minutes to 1 hour and 45 minutes).

6   Carefully transfer the chickens to a platter to rest. Pour off the liquid from the pan into a glass measuring cup, leaving the onions and necks in the pan. Using a spoon or baster, skim off as much fat as possible from the liquid. The onions should have browned while cooking under the chicken, but in case they haven't, place the roasting pan over medium-high heat until they brown.

7   Pour the wine into the pan and deglaze over medium-high heat; loosen the brown bits from the bottom of the pan with a wooden spoon. Add the remaining 2 cups of stock and bring to a boil. Remove from the heat. Pour the liquid from the roasting pan into a sieve set over a medium saucepan, pressing down on the onions to release the juices. Set the onions aside and discard the necks.

8   Add the skimmed liquid that was set aside from step 6 to the saucepan, as well as the juices that have accumulated on the plate under the chickens. Bring to a boil over high heat and cook until the liquid has reduced by one fourth.

9   Combine the remaining 2 tablespoons butter and the flour in a small bowl, making a thick paste. Whisk the flour-butter paste into the sauce, whisking continuously, until it is dissolved. Bring to a boil and simmer for 5 minutes. Just before serving, add a few pinches of finely chopped rosemary and a few of the reserved onions, if desired, and season with salt and pepper to taste.

10   Remove the toothpicks and strings from the chickens. Scoop out the stuffing into a large serving bowl and sprinkle with parsley leaves and the remaining pomegranate seeds. Carve the chickens and serve immediately with the gravy.

> I always make a small bowl of a mixture of salt and freshly ground pepper (about a 2-to-1 ratio) when I make any roast chicken. That way, I can season the cavity with only one hand (the other is busy holding on to the chicken) and don't have to worry about gunking up my peppermill or contaminating my bowl of salt.

SEEDING A POMEGRANATE   To seed a pomegranate, cut it into quarters. Using your fingers, gently scoop out the juicy seeds, and discard everything else. To make this a neater job, scoop out the seeds with the fruit submerged in a bowl of cold water. Then drain the water out and use the seeds.

PAPRIKA ROAST CHICKEN WITH ROOT VEGETABLES

SERVES 2

1 whole chicken (about 3½ pounds), neck
    reserved

3 tablespoons smoked paprika
    (see page 89)

¼ teaspoon cayenne pepper

2 teaspoons dried thyme

Kosher salt and freshly ground black pepper

½ lemon

2 thyme sprigs

4 carrots, cut into 3-inch pieces

4 parsnips, cut into 3-inch pieces

1 small celeriac (celery root), peeled
    and cut into 1-inch wedges

2 shallots, cut lengthwise into quarters

1 tablespoon olive oil

1 small onion, cut into 4 thick slices

I used to think that paprika was what you put on chicken when you didn't know what else to do, but I have come to appreciate the subtle differences in flavor among the different types. Smoked paprika, or pimentón, is a great discovery and elevates a roast chicken to new heights. Sweet Hungarian paprika can also be used. If you want, the chicken can be prepared through step 2 up to a day ahead of time. Store the vegetables separately, and leave the chicken to marinate in a resealable plastic bag.

1 Wash and dry the chicken. Remove and discard the excess fat around the neck area. Transfer the chicken to a large piece of parchment or wax paper. In a small bowl, combine the paprika, cayenne, dried thyme, and 1 teaspoon salt. Season the chicken inside and out with salt and pepper. Place the half lemon and thyme sprigs inside the chicken. Using your hands, massage the dry rub onto the chicken, making sure to coat the entire bird, including the bottom.

2 Combine the carrots, parsnips, celeriac, and shallots in a large bowl. Drizzle the oil over the vegetables and season with ½ teaspoon salt and pepper to taste. Toss well.

3 Preheat the oven to 450°F. In a large roasting pan, arrange the onion slices in a single layer. They should be pushed together in the center of the pan and should cover just enough area to fit under the chicken, to serve as a roasting rack for the chicken. Add the chicken neck to the roasting pan, if you have it.

4 Transfer the chicken to the "onion rack" in the roasting pan. Arrange the vegetables around the chicken and place the pan in the oven.

5 After 15 minutes, turn the vegetables and reduce the oven temperature to 350°F. Roast until the legs of the chicken move easily when wiggled and an instant-read thermometer registers 180°F when inserted into the thickest part of the thigh (1 hour and 15 minutes to 1 hour and 30 minutes), turning the vegetables every 15 minutes. Remove from the oven and allow to rest for 15 minutes. Carve the bird, and serve with the vegetables and pan juices, if desired.

> ### HOW TO CARVE A CHICKEN:

It's a pretty messy job, and it helps to have a carving board with a well to catch the juices. If you don't, place some folded paper towels around the edges of your cutting board so the juices don't run all over the counter.

1   Remove the wings by gently twisting them off.

2   Remove the breasts by cutting down along the center breastbone, and then down along the ribs, keeping your knife as close to the bone as possible. (The best knife to use is a flexible one with a thin blade, such as a boning knife or slicing knife.) Cut the breasts crosswise into slices, as thick or as thin as you want them, keeping the breast in its original shape and the skin intact.

3   Gently pull the entire leg (including thigh) away from the body using the knife to help you, and with your knife, find the hip joint. Separate the joint by working the knife in between the two parts. You don't need to cut through any bones.

4   Do the same thing to separate the drumstick from the thigh: Find the joint, and separate the two parts, keeping the skin intact.

5   Arrange all of the parts attractively on a warm platter. Pour any juices that have run out over the meat and serve.

RESTING MEAT   When cooking meat or poultry by roasting, searing, or grilling, it is best to let it rest for about 10 minutes before cutting or serving it. This resting time will allow the juices to redistribute throughout the meat, rather than running out in a torrent. It will also allow time for "carryover" cooking, which means that the meat will continue to cook a bit after it's been removed from the heat source, so always take it off just a little ahead of when it's done. By the end of the resting period, the meat will be juicy and perfect and easy to carve or slice.

SERVES 6

6 boneless, skinless chicken breast halves
(about 3 pounds)

Kosher salt and freshly ground black pepper

1 head Roasted Garlic (page 21), optional

18 very thin slices of pancetta

16 large sage leaves

4 large russet (baking) potatoes (about
3 pounds total), scrubbed

1 lemon, cut in half

4 tablespoons olive oil, plus more for
drizzling

½ cup dry white wine

1 cup Golden Chicken Stock (page 178)

Coarse sea salt

Boneless chicken breasts get a little special treatment, rendering them fit for company, but this recipe is so easy, you might make it a family regular. Roasted garlic adds loads of flavor, but this dish is perfectly delicious without it, too.

1   Wash and dry the chicken. Remove the tenderloin and set aside for another use. Season both sides lightly with kosher salt and pepper. Using a fork, spread the roasted garlic, if using, all over the chicken breasts. On the top side of the breast, lay 1 slice of pancetta over the lower portion of the breast, wrapping it snugly so it adheres. Lay a sage leaf on the center of the breast, and wrap the upper portion with a second slice of pancetta. Turn the breast over and wrap a third slice of pancetta over the back of the breast. Repeat with the remaining chicken, transferring the pieces to a plate as you go. (The chicken can be made in advance up to this point. Just wrap tightly in plastic wrap and refrigerate.)

2   Preheat the oven to 450°F and position one rack in the lower third of the oven and one in the upper third. Slice the potatoes lengthwise into ¼- to ½-inch slices, then cut the slices into ¼-inch-thick fries.

3   Toss the potatoes, lemon, 10 sage leaves, oil, and a pinch of kosher salt and pepper in a large bowl until well coated. Arrange the potatoes in a single layer on a large baking sheet and transfer to the lower oven rack for 15 minutes. Gently stir and rearrange the potatoes so they brown evenly and return to the oven until they are browned on all sides, tossing several times, about 30 minutes more.

4   Meanwhile, heat a large cast-iron skillet or grill pan over high heat until it is very hot. Drizzle the pancetta-wrapped chicken with oil and place in the pan with the sage leaf side down. Cook over high heat until the pancetta is brown, about 5 minutes. Turn the breasts over and transfer the pan to the upper rack of the oven for 15 minutes, or until cooked through.

5 Remove the chicken from the pan, transfer to a plate, and set aside. Deglaze the pan with the wine over high heat. Reduce the wine until almost evaporated, and add the chicken stock. Continue to cook until reduced by half.

6 Transfer the chicken and potatoes to a large platter. Squeeze any juice left in the lemon halves over the potatoes and sprinkle them with coarse sea salt. Serve potatoes and chicken on a large platter with the pan juices on the side and Spicy Braised Broccoli Rabe (page 308).

> Pancetta is pork belly that has been cured but not smoked, with spices and salt for several months. The pancetta for this recipe should be sliced thin but not paper-thin. Don't be shy when you are in the store. Ask the deli person to show you a slice. You should be able to wrap it around your hand, and have it stick. If you can see through it, it is too thin. If it is too thick to wrap around your hand and stick by itself, it is too thick.

PORK TONNATO

SERVES 8 TO 10

FOR THE ROAST

1 boneless center-cut pork loin (3 pounds)

1 tablespoon finely chopped rosemary

1 tablespoon finely chopped garlic

1 teaspoon kosher salt

½ teaspoon freshly ground black pepper

8 thin slices prosciutto (about 4 ounces)

FOR THE SAUCE

1 can (6 ounces) light tuna packed in oil,
     preferably Italian, undrained

2 tablespoons capers, rinsed

1 teaspoon anchovy paste, or 1 or 2
     anchovy fillets

Juice of 1 lemon

1 small or ½ large garlic clove

Kosher salt and freshly ground black pepper

¼ cup mayonnaise

½ cup extra virgin olive oil

1 tablespoon flat-leaf parsley leaves

FOR SERVING

½ pound haricots verts or green beans

3 tablespoons extra virgin olive oil

Juice of ½ lemon

Coarse sea salt and freshly ground
     black pepper

1 Roasted Pepper (page 23), sliced into
     thin strips

Capers, optional

This is a twist on vitello tonnato, *the classic Italian dish of sliced cold veal accompanied by a tuna-mayonnaise sauce, that is enjoying a bit of a revival. It is a make-ahead dish, perfect for a summer's lunch or dinner. Plan ahead; this does take two days to prepare. Accompany with a bowl of spicy arugula, some olives, and a loaf of crusty bread. Use a veal loin if you wish, but pork makes this an economical dish.*

1   Preheat the oven to 375°F. If the roast is tied, remove the string. Combine the rosemary, garlic, salt, and pepper on a cutting board and chop together. Make a paste by rubbing it all together with the side of a large knife. Rub the paste over all sides of the pork. Wrap the roast with the prosciutto and place on a roasting rack in a roasting pan with the fattier side of the roast facing up. Let stand for 15 minutes at room temperature. Place the pan in the oven and roast for about 1 hour, or until the internal temperature reaches between 140° and 150°F. Transfer to a plate and let rest at room temperature for 1 hour. Cover in plastic wrap and refrigerate overnight.

2   Combine the tuna with its oil, the capers, anchovy paste, lemon juice, garlic, a pinch of salt and pepper, and the mayonnaise in a mini food processor or blender. Blend for a few seconds to combine. Continue to blend while slowly drizzling in the oil. Add the parsley and blend for a few more seconds. This can be done up to several days ahead of time. Store in an airtight container in the refrigerator.

3   Slice the pork loin as thinly as possible. Spread a layer of the sauce on a large flat platter. Arrange the pork on top of the sauce in an overlapping circle, leaving room in the center. Cover tightly with plastic wrap and refrigerate if not serving right away.

4   Just before serving, remove the pork from the refrigerator. Blanch the haricots verts in boiling salted water for 1 to 2 minutes, until bright green. Drain and plunge into ice water. Drain well, blotting with a paper towel. Dress the haricots verts with the oil, lemon juice, and salt and pepper to taste. Pile the haricots verts and roasted pepper in the middle of the platter and sprinkle with capers, if using. Serve any extra sauce on the side.

ROAST FILLET OF BEEF WITH MUSHROOM SAUCE

SERVES 4 TO 6

1 fillet of beef (2 pounds), silverskin removed

Kosher salt and freshly ground black pepper

1 tablespoon olive oil, plus more for pan

1 tablespoon plus 1 teaspoon unsalted butter

4 ounces cremini mushrooms, trimmed and thickly sliced

4 ounces oyster mushrooms, trimmed and thickly sliced

4 ounces shiitake mushrooms, stems removed and thickly sliced

1 medium shallot, minced

½ cup Madeira

1 cup Brown Veal Stock (page 179) or low-sodium beef stock

A fillet of beef, also called tenderloin, is an elegant roast that's quick and easy to cook as long as you use an instant-read thermometer rather than guesswork to make sure it isn't overcooked. Even five minutes can mean the difference between perfect medium-rare and ruinous well-done. The sauce depends on a good Brown Veal Stock (page 179). Serve with Basic Popovers with herbs (page 161), Potato-Celeriac Mash (page 198), or Rosemary-Roasted Potatoes (page 142).

1   Preheat the oven to 375°F. Season the beef with salt and pepper on all sides.

2   Heat a large cast-iron skillet until hot. Coat lightly with oil, and sear the meat on all sides until well browned all over, 8 to 10 minutes. Transfer skillet to the oven and roast until the meat reaches an internal temperature of 130°F, for medium-rare, about 25 minutes. Transfer to a cutting board and let the meat rest 10 minutes before slicing.

3   Meanwhile, sauté the mushrooms: Heat 1 teaspoon oil and 1 teaspoon of the butter over high heat in a frying pan large enough to accommodate the mushrooms without crowding. Add the cremini mushrooms and season with a pinch of salt and pepper. Sauté until golden brown, tossing frequently, 5 to 7 minutes. Transfer to a plate and set aside.

4   Add 1 teaspoon oil and 1 teaspoon butter to the pan and sauté the oyster mushrooms. Add to the creminis and set aside. Repeat process with the shiitake mushrooms and set aside.

5   Add the remaining 1 teaspoon butter and the minced shallot to the pan. Sauté over medium heat, stirring frequently, until the shallot has softened but has not begun to brown, about 2 minutes. Add the Madeira and cook until it has reduced to a glaze, about 3 minutes. Add the veal stock and cook until slightly thickened, about 5 minutes. Season with salt and pepper to taste.

6   Just before serving, reheat all the mushrooms in a hot frying pan for a few seconds. Slice the meat into medallions and arrange on a platter. Arrange the mushrooms all around the roast, and pour the sauce over the meat, or serve on the side in a warm sauceboat.

SERVES 6

2 bunches carrots (about 16)

5 thyme sprigs

2 tablespoons extra virgin olive oil

Coarse sea salt and freshly ground

    black pepper

Since decent carrots are available year-round, we don't really think of them as having a season, but they do. Late fall, after the first frost and once the ground gets nice and cold, is when carrots become their sweetest. I like to use fresh bunch carrots rather than bagged ones for roasting, since they tend to be more slender and uniform. Leave about an inch or two of the stem attached for a nice presentation.

1 | Preheat the oven to 425°F. Peel the carrots, leaving the tips and 1 inch of the stems intact. Cut larger carrots in half lengthwise. The carrots should all be approximately the same size and thickness so they roast evenly.

2 | Coat the carrots and thyme with the oil on a large baking sheet or shallow roasting pan. Season with salt and pepper. Arrange them on the pan so that they are evenly spaced and not crowded. Roast, shaking the pan occasionally, until the carrots turn deep golden brown all over, about 45 minutes.

> Thyme leaves don't need to be picked off the stems for this recipe. Most of the leaves will fall from the stems, which can then be discarded before serving.

SERVES 6

2½ pounds small potatoes, such as red or
yellow creamers, fingerlings, or baby
Yukon golds

10 garlic cloves, unpeeled

2 tablespoons extra virgin olive oil

¼ cup rosemary leaves

½ teaspoon kosher salt

Freshly ground black pepper

Sea salt, for sprinkling

A shallow aluminum baking pan (nine by thirteen inches) is best for roasting potatoes. The shallow profile allows for efficient browning, and its lightness makes it easy to shake with one hand. Scatter whole, unpeeled garlic cloves to infuse the potatoes with their flavor. Serve the roasted garlic cloves in their skins.

1 Preheat the oven to 425°F. Wash and dry the potatoes. Cut ones larger than a golf ball into halves or quarters.

2 Toss the potatoes, garlic, oil, rosemary, kosher salt, and pepper in a roasting or baking pan, making sure the potatoes are evenly coated. Arrange the potatoes with the cut sides down. Transfer to the oven.

3 Once the cut sides begin to brown, about 30 minutes, shake the pan and turn the potatoes with a large spatula. Return to the oven and continue to roast until all sides are golden brown and begin to crisp, shaking every 10 minutes, about another 30 minutes. Transfer to a serving bowl and sprinkle with sea salt to taste.

SERVES 4 TO 6

4 mixed winter squash, about the same size

2-inch piece ginger, peeled

2 tablespoons unsalted butter

¼ cup honey

½ teaspoon kosher salt

In the fall a dazzling selection of small, thin-skinned winter squash is available at markets and farm stands. They're ideal for roasting and they all take about the same amount of time to cook. Look for Acorn, Sweet Dumpling, Delicata, and Carnival varieties. Serve with Sunday Chicken with Couscous Stuffing (page 128) or with your Thanksgiving turkey.

1   Preheat the oven to 450°F, and position a rack in the middle of the oven. Cut each squash in half and scoop out the seeds and fibrous flesh from inside. Then cut larger ones in half again. Transfer to a large bowl and set aside.

2   Thinly slice the ginger, then cut it into thin matchsticks and set aside. In a small saucepan, melt the butter and honey. Add ¼ cup water and the ginger and stir well. Pour the butter and honey mixture over the squash and toss well, making sure that all the squash pieces are well coated. Sprinkle the salt over the squash and toss.

3   Spread the squash evenly on a baking sheet and transfer to the oven. Bake 45 minutes to 1 hour, turning and basting the squash every 10 to 15 minutes. Add a few tablespoons of water as the squash roasts if it seems to be burning. The squash should be golden brown and very soft.

BAKE

LIKE ROASTING, BAKING IS A DRY-HEAT OVEN METHOD. NO HARD AND FAST RULES DISTINGUISH

one from the other, although baking is most often done at temperatures that range from 325° to 375°F.

Savory baked dishes are ideal candidates for casual entertaining or family gatherings. They can usually be assembled ahead of time and kept in the refrigerator until ready to cook and serve. All that's left for you to do is pop them in the oven and get dressed, while the enticing smells fill the house just in time to greet your guests. It also happens that baked dishes, or the kind I crave anyway, are particularly comforting and nurturing. Rigatoni with Squash and Caramelized Onions (page 166) fits the bill.

Not all baked dishes are casserole-y comfort food, though. Baking is one of the simplest and fastest ways to cook fish. One very good reason to bake fish fillets, such as the Baked Grouper with Blood Oranges (page 170), is that they can be prepared completely ahead of time, save for a trip to the hot oven for twenty minutes or so. Another advantage of cooking fish in the gentle heat of the oven is that your house won't smell like fish. By the way, a rule of thumb for cooking fish in the oven, or anywhere for that matter, is to allow ten minutes of cooking time per inch of thickness at the thickest point.

An oven is like a Jack-in-the-Box; even though we've seen it a million times, it's still exciting to see a freshly baked pizza or billowy popovers emerge, or a parchment pouch that you carefully pleated puff up and brown.

Baking is a user-friendly method. More than with any other technique, the food tells you when it is ready, by browning to a perfectly toasted golden color, bubbling around the edges, and emitting intoxicating aromas.

ITALIAN SHEPHERD'S PIE

4 tablespoons olive oil, plus more for
coating garlic

2 large red onions, cut in half lengthwise
and sliced ½ inch thick

4 thyme sprigs

Kosher salt and freshly ground black pepper

4 plum tomatoes

2 zucchini, sliced on the diagonal about
¼ inch thick

2 yellow squash or yellow zucchini, sliced on
the diagonal about ¼ inch thick

1 red pepper, cored and seeded, cut into
¾-inch strips

1 tablespoon red wine or balsamic vinegar

3 or 4 garlic cloves, very thinly sliced

1 cup freshly grated Parmigiano-Reggiano

This dish is named for the French Provençal vessel it is traditionally cooked in, but any shallow ceramic, glass, copper, or earthenware baking dish is fine. If you use a smaller or larger dish than the one called for, you may have to adjust the amount of vegetables. The vegetables should overlap one another by about half. If there are too many vegetables in too small a dish, the final results will be soupy. Leftovers are great crisped in a hot pan. Small, firm zucchini and squash will be less watery.

1   Preheat the oven to 375°F. Heat 1 tablespoon oil in a large frying pan. Add the onions, the leaves of 2 thyme sprigs, and salt and pepper to taste. Cook over medium-high heat until the onions begin to wilt and turn brown, about 10 minutes. If they begin to burn, turn down the heat. Set aside.

2   Meanwhile, slice off the bottoms of the tomatoes and gently squeeze out the seeds. Cut into ¼-inch slices, discarding the top stem slice. Combine the zucchini, squash, red pepper, and tomatoes in a large bowl. Toss with 3 tablespoons oil, the vinegar, and salt and pepper.

3   Spread the onions on the bottom of a large (about 10 inches) baking dish. Arrange each vegetable in rows on top of the onions. Very lightly coat the garlic with oil and sprinkle over the tian. Sprinkle the leaves of the remaining 2 thyme sprigs and the cheese over the top. Bake for 35 to 45 minutes, until the top is golden brown and all the vegetables are tender.

RADICCHIO AND PROSCIUTTO PIZZA

MAKES FOUR 10-INCH PIZZAS

Basic Pizza Dough (page 154)

4 to 8 tablespoons cornmeal

8 to 12 thin slices prosciutto (about 10 ounces)

About 2 cups shredded radicchio

About 6 ounces mozzarella or Italian fontina, cut into 4 equal pieces

Extra virgin olive oil, for brushing crust

Radicchio makes a good pizza topping since it doesn't require any precooking. It will lose some of its color in the oven, but not its flavor.

1 Cut the dough into 4 equal pieces and shape each portion into a round. Cover and let rest 10 minutes. In the meantime, position a pizza stone or oven rack as low in the oven as possible. Preheat the oven to 475°F.

2 Sprinkle 1 to 2 tablespoons cornmeal in a 10-inch pizza pan, on a large baking sheet, or on a pizza peel if using a stone. Stretch the dough into a circle approximately 10 inches in diameter and no more than ¼ inch thick. Lay the dough on the prepared surface and repair any holes by pinching the dough together.

3 Lay 2 or 3 pieces of prosciutto on the pizza. Then spread about ½ cup of the radicchio evenly over the entire surface of dough, leaving ¼ inch of dough to form the edge of the pizza. Slice 1 piece of cheese into uniform slices and put on top of radicchio. Lightly brush the exposed crust with olive oil.

4 Transfer the pizza to the oven and bake 15 to 18 minutes, until the edge of the pizza is golden brown and the cheese is bubbling. Repeat with the remaining 3 dough rounds. Serve them as they come out, or keep warm until ready to serve. You can also bake 2 at a time.

MAKES FOUR 10-INCH PIZZAS

Basic Pizza Dough (page 154)

4 to 8 tablespoons coarse cornmeal

About 6 ounces mozzarella cheese,
    cut into 4 equal pieces

About 1 cup grape or cherry tomatoes,
    cut in half

1 heaping tablespoon fresh oregano leaves

Extra virgin olive oil, for brushing crust

This classic combination is hard to beat. Use any kind of small tomato (there are so many good ones these days) and you'll get lots of juicy tomato flavor, but they won't be too wet. You can also use Slow-Roasted Tomatoes (page 24).

1   Cut the dough into 4 equal pieces and shape each portion into a round. Cover and let rest 10 minutes. Position a pizza stone or oven rack as low in the oven as possible. Preheat the oven to 475°F.

2   Sprinkle 1 to 2 tablespoons cornmeal in a 10-inch pizza pan, on a large baking sheet, or on a pizza peel if using a stone. Stretch the dough evenly into a circle approximately 10 inches in diameter and no more than ¼ inch thick. Lay the dough on the prepared surface and repair any holes by pinching the dough together.

3   Take one piece of cheese, slice into uniform pieces, and spread it out evenly on top of the dough. Arrange about ¼ cup tomatoes on the pizza, leaving a ¼-inch border. Sprinkle about 1 teaspoon oregano leaves over the top. Lightly brush the exposed crust with olive oil.

4   Transfer the pizza to the oven and bake 15 to 18 minutes, until the edge of the pizza is golden brown and the cheese is bubbling. Repeat with the remaining 3 dough rounds. Serve them as they come out, or keep warm until ready to serve. You can also bake 2 at a time.

MAKES FOUR 10-INCH PIZZAS

Basic Pizza Dough (page 154)

1 tablespoon extra virgin olive oil, plus more
for brushing crust

1 tablespoon unsalted butter

2 packages (10 ounces each) mushrooms,
trimmed and sliced ¼ inch thick

Kosher salt and freshly ground black pepper

4 to 8 tablespoons coarse cornmeal

About 6 ounces Taleggio, cut into 4 equal
pieces

1 cup ricotta

½ cup crisped bacon or pancetta pieces

1 tablespoon coarsely chopped rosemary
leaves

Taleggio is a semisoft Italian cheese that turns thin and milky when melted. It is good combined with other cheeses such as mozzarella or fontina or ricotta.

1   Cut the dough into 4 equal pieces and shape each portion into a round. Cover and let rest 10 minutes. Position a pizza stone or oven rack as low in the oven as possible. Preheat the oven to 475°F.

2   Heat 1 tablespoon each oil and butter in a large frying pan until hot. Add the mushrooms and a pinch of salt and pepper, and sauté over high heat until the mushrooms turn golden brown, about 10 minutes. Set aside.

3   Sprinkle 1 to 2 tablespoons cornmeal in a 10-inch pizza pan, on a large baking sheet, or on a pizza peel if using a stone. Stretch the dough into a circle approximately 10 inches in diameter and no more than ¼ inch thick. Lay the dough on the prepared surface and repair any holes by pinching the dough together.

4   Slice 1 piece of Taleggio into uniform pieces and place evenly on the entire surface of the dough, leaving ¼ inch of dough to form the edge of the pizza. Spoon ¼ cup of the ricotta in dollops over the surface of the dough and then sprinkle one quarter of the mushrooms over the cheeses. Sprinkle with one quarter of the bacon and rosemary. Lightly brush the exposed crust with olive oil.

5   Transfer the pizza to the oven and bake 15 to 18 minutes, until the edge of the pizza is golden brown and the cheese is bubbling. Repeat with the remaining 3 dough rounds. Serve them as they come out, or keep warm until ready to serve. You can also bake 2 at a time.

ROSEMARY FOCACCIA

MAKES 1 LOAF

1 package active dry yeast

¼ teaspoon sugar

About ¾ cup extra virgin olive oil, plus more for coating pan

1½ teaspoons kosher salt

3 cups plus 2 tablespoons all-purpose flour, plus more for kneading

Coarse sea salt

About 3 tablespoons rosemary leaves

This easy-to-make Italian flatbread is famous for its pockets of olive oil, which form when the dough is dimpled with your fingertips, so make sure you use a tasty extra virgin oil here. Serve this warm from the oven if possible. It can be eaten on the second day, but heat it up first. Serve as an appetizer with antipasto, or alongside soups and salads.

1   Fill the metal bowl of an electric stand mixer with hot water then pour it out and dry. This will warm the bowl.

2   In the warmed bowl, combine the yeast, sugar, and 1 cup warm (100° to 110°F) water. Stir well to dissolve the yeast. Let stand for 5 to 10 minutes until foam appears.

3   Add ½ cup warm water, ¼ cup oil, and the kosher salt. Mix for a few seconds with the paddle attachment. Slowly add the flour. Continue to mix on medium speed for about 7 minutes. The dough will be wet and will not form a ball.

4   Generously coat a 9- × 13-inch baking pan with oil. Turn the dough into the prepared pan and spread the dough using your fingers. If it is too sticky, put a few drops of oil on your hands. It is not necessary to spread the dough all the way to the edges. As the dough rises it will spread and fill the pan. Cover with plastic wrap. Let the dough rise until it has doubled in volume, about 2 hours.

5   Preheat the oven to 425°F and position a rack in the middle of the oven. Using well-oiled fingers, dimple the dough all over. Pour about ½ cup oil over the dough and dimple again so that the holes fill with oil. Sprinkle with coarse sea salt and rosemary leaves. Bake until deep golden brown, about 25 minutes. Immediately remove the focaccia from the pan and transfer to a wire rack. Cool slightly.

>   Spray the plastic wrap used to cover the dough in step 4 with cooking spray so it doesn't stick to the dough.

BASIC POPOVERS

MAKES 6 TO 8

1 cup all-purpose flour, plus more for
   dusting tin

1 teaspoon kosher salt

2 large eggs, at room temperature

1 cup warm milk

1½ tablespoons unsalted butter, melted,
   plus more for greasing tin

About 1 tablespoon chopped fresh herbs,
   optional

Popovers can be made in a variety of sizes—use a popover pan for very large ones, a standard muffin tin for slightly smaller ones, even a mini-muffin tin for hors d'oeuvre size. The batter rises best when chilled overnight but they can be baked right away, too. Add one tablespoon chopped fresh herbs such as thyme or chives for savory popovers to serve with Roast Fillet of Beef with Mushroom Sauce (page 138) or make the basic batter and serve them with butter and jam at brunch.

1 | Whisk together the flour and salt in a small bowl and set aside.

2 | Whisk the eggs in a medium bowl. Slowly whisk in the milk and butter. Pour the flour mixture into the egg mixture and whisk until smooth. Add the fresh herbs, if using. Cover with plastic wrap and refrigerate 6 hours or overnight.

3 | Preheat the oven to 450°F and position a rack in the middle of the oven. Brush a muffin or popover pan with melted butter and dust with flour.

4 | Stir the batter well. Fill each cup three-quarters full with batter; fill unused cups one third full with water so they don't burn. Immediately transfer to the oven and bake for 15 minutes. Reduce temperature to 350°F and bake until well browned and crusty, about 20 minutes. Remove from the oven and serve immediately.

MAKES 2½ DOZEN

1 cup all-purpose flour, plus more for
   dusting tin

1 teaspoon kosher salt

2 ounces cheese

2 large eggs, room temperature

1 cup warm milk

1½ tablespoons unsalted butter, melted,
   plus more for greasing tin

1 tablespoon chopped fresh herbs, optional

Use whatever cheese you like for these hors d'oeuvre–size popovers. Try Gruyère, Comté, any kind of blue cheese, Cheddar, or goat. Serve them piping hot in a basket or bowl lined with a napkin.

1 | Whisk together the flour and salt in a small bowl and set aside. Grate the cheese or cut it into very small cubes and set aside.

2 | Whisk the eggs in a medium bowl. Slowly whisk in the milk and the butter. Pour the flour mixture into the egg mixture and whisk until smooth. Add the cheese and herbs, if using, and stir. Cover with plastic wrap and refrigerate 6 hours or overnight.

3 | Preheat the oven to 450°F and position a rack in the middle of the oven. Brush a mini-popover pan with melted butter and dust with flour.

4 | Stir the batter well. Fill each cup three-quarters full with batter; fill unused cups one-third full with water so they don't burn. Immediately transfer to the oven and bake until well browned and crusty, about 18 minutes. Remove from the oven and serve immediately.

SERVES 4 AS A SIDE DISH OR APPETIZER

1 pound mixed mushrooms, such as
  shiitake, oyster, and cremini

4 thyme sprigs

2 tablespoons low-sodium soy sauce

¼ teaspoon kosher salt

2 pinches of freshly ground black pepper

2 teaspoons unsalted butter, cut into small
  pieces

1 head Roasted Garlic (page 21)

Even cultivated mushrooms take on a deep, complex flavor when cooked in these flavor-sealing packets. A tiny bit of butter goes a long way in permeating the mushrooms. Purchase a variety of small mushrooms, so they can be left whole. Open the packages at the table for a dramatic touch. Top sharply dressed, slightly bitter greens with these mushrooms for an easy and elegant first course. Crisped-up leftovers tossed into an omelet make a fine breakfast.

1   Preheat the oven to 400°F. Tear off two 24-inch lengths of parchment paper. With the long side facing you, fold each piece of paper in half vertically. Using a pair of scissors, cut the folded parchment into a half-heart shape and set aside.

2   Clean the mushrooms (see below). Remove the stems from the shiitake mushrooms and cut caps larger than 2 inches into halves or quarters. Separate oyster mushrooms into individual stems, removing the root if large. Trim the stems on the cremini mushrooms and slice into ¼-inch slices.

3   Open the parchment "hearts" and divide the mushrooms and thyme evenly between the 2 packets, placing them in the center of one half of the heart. Sprinkle the soy sauce, salt, and pepper evenly over the mushrooms in the 2 packets; dab on the butter and garlic.

4   Fold the parchment over and seal the edges with a series of long overlapping folds, starting in the "cleavage" of the heart. It is important to make sure no openings remain for steam to escape. On the last fold at the point, tightly twist the end and tuck under the packet. At this point, they can be refrigerated for several hours.

5   Place the parchment packages on a baking sheet and bake for about 30 minutes, until the parchment puffs and you can hear the mushrooms sizzling. Using a sharp knife or scissors, cut next to the folds and peel back. Discard the thyme, gently stir the mushrooms, and serve immediately.

MUSHROOMS Many chefs and cookbooks instruct cooks not to wash mushrooms, but rather wipe or brush them to remove dirt, claiming that, if washed, they will become waterlogged and then be hard to cook properly. I don't find this to be practical, and for the most part, I do wash mushrooms if they are so sandy or dirty that there's no way around it. If possible, wipe them with a damp paper towel. If they need more thorough cleaning, wash them very quickly a few at a time in a mesh sieve, and then spread them out on paper towels. Blot them to absorb excess water, and let them air-dry as long as possible before cooking so that any water they've absorbed can evaporate.

RIGATONI WITH SQUASH AND CARAMELIZED ONIONS

SERVES 8 TO 10

Kosher salt

1 pound small rigatoni

1 large or 2 small butternut squash
(about 4 pounds total)

2 ¼-inch-thick slices pancetta (about 4
ounces total), cubed

3 garlic cloves, thinly sliced

1 tablespoon unsalted butter

2 large onions, cut in half lengthwise and
thickly sliced

Freshly ground black pepper

1 tablespoon olive oil

2 tablespoons rosemary leaves, finely
chopped

1½ cups Golden Chicken Stock (page 178) or
vegetable stock

1½ cups heavy cream

About 1½ cups freshly grated Parmigiano-
Reggiano

½ pound Italian fontina, cut into ½-inch
pieces

All of my favorite fall flavors are combined in this incredibly rich and totally-worth-the-time-it-takes-to-prepare pasta dish (though it can be done up to a day ahead of time). It's absolutely perfect for a casual weekend buffet. Serve it with a big, crisp salad of spicy greens, and it's all you need. Choose a light dessert like Roasted Pears with Red Wine (page 248) with this.

1   Bring a large pot of water to a boil. Add 1 teaspoon salt and the pasta to the water. Cook the pasta according to package directions, stirring occasionally, until just short of al dente; the pasta should still be white at the center when cut in half. (It will continue to cook in the oven.) Drain and rinse the pasta; set aside.

2   While the water is coming to a boil, cut the squash in half crosswise, separating the neck from the ball. Peel and seed both halves of the squash. Cut into ¾-inch chunks and set aside. Cook the pancetta in a 12-inch sauté pan (preferably nonstick) over medium-high heat, stirring frequently, until crisp and brown, about 10 minutes. Remove with a slotted spoon, transfer to a plate, and set aside.

3   Leaving 2 tablespoons of fat in the pan, add the garlic and sauté until golden brown, stirring frequently, about 5 minutes. Add the butter and onions and cook until golden brown, stirring occasionally, about 10 minutes. Reduce the heat to low, season with salt and pepper. Add ¼ cup water, cover, and cook for 5 more minutes. Remove the onions from the pan to a large bowl and set aside.

4   Add the oil, squash, half of the chopped rosemary, ½ teaspoon salt, and ¼ teaspoon pepper to the sauté pan and cook over high heat, stirring frequently, until tender when pierced with a paring knife, about 10 minutes. Add the stock and bring to a boil; reduce to a simmer and cook over medium heat. Cook until the squash has absorbed most of the liquid and is quite tender, 8 to 10 minutes, and the liquid that remains in the pan has thickened. If the squash is not tender add some additional water and continue to simmer until tender. Add the cream and bring to a boil. Boil for 1 minute; remove from the heat.

5 Transfer the squash to a large bowl and cool slightly, stirring occasionally. Add the pasta, half of the onions, the pancetta, 1 cup of the Parmigiano, the fontina, and the remainder of the rosemary. Season with salt and pepper to taste. Stir gently to combine thoroughly. Transfer to a 4-quart baking dish and spread the remaining onions over the top. If baking right away, proceed to step 6. Otherwise, cover tightly with plastic wrap and refrigerate until ready to bake. The pasta can be made to this point up to one day in advance.

6 Preheat the oven to 350°F. Sprinkle about ½ cup Parmigiano over the top and transfer to the oven. Bake for about 45 minutes, until the top is golden brown and the sauce is bubbling. Serve immediately.

> **To save some prep time, buy the peeled and cubed butternut squash from the supermarket produce section.**

SERVES 6 TO 8

FOR THE STEW

3 pounds lamb stew meat, cut into
    1-inch pieces

Kosher salt and freshly ground black pepper

2 to 3 tablespoons extra virgin olive oil

2 garlic cloves, chopped

2 small onions, coarsely chopped

2 small eggplant, cut into ½-inch cubes,
    about 2 cups

1 bay leaf

1 thyme sprig

1 rosemary sprig

1½ cups red wine

3 tablespoons tomato paste

4 cups low-sodium beef stock or water

FOR THE GNOCCHI TOPPING

1 quart milk

¼ teaspoon ground nutmeg

½ teaspoon kosher salt

1 cup semolina

2 large egg yolks

2 tablespoons unsalted butter

1 cup freshly grated Parmigiano-Reggiano

This hearty, make-ahead party dish is inspired by moussaka, the classic Greek dish with eggplant, lamb, and béchamel, and by shepherd's pie—lamb or beef stew topped with mashed potatoes. The topping is a creamy semolina dumpling, which is reminiscent of the béchamel topping of moussaka. This makes a very satisfying cold weather meal. The whole dish can be assembled ahead of time, refrigerated, and then baked. (See photograph on page 151.)

1 Blot the lamb with paper towels to remove excess moisture. Season with salt and pepper immediately before browning. (If browning in batches, wait to season each batch until just before it goes in the pan.) Heat 1 tablespoon of the oil in a large Dutch oven over high heat. Brown the meat in a single layer, making sure not to crowd the pan. Cook until the liquid has evaporated and the meat is brown on all sides, stirring occasionally, 15 to 20 minutes. Transfer to a plate and continue to brown the remaining lamb, adding 1 tablespoon of oil for each batch.

2 Once all the meat has been browned and set aside, add the garlic and onions to the pan. Sauté over medium-high heat until transparent, stirring frequently, about 5 minutes. Add the eggplant, and cook for 3 minutes, stirring occasionally. Return the meat to the pot and add the bay leaf, thyme, rosemary, wine, and tomato paste. Stir well until the ingredients are well combined and the tomato paste is dissolved. Add the stock, season with salt and pepper, and bring to a boil. Reduce to a slow but steady simmer and cook, uncovered, until the juices have thickened and the meat is very tender, about 2 hours. Stir occasionally. If the juices haven't thickened enough, turn the heat up to medium-high and reduce it until thick, about 10 to 15 minutes more. Remove the bay leaf and herb sprigs. (At this point the stew can be stored in an airtight container for up to 2 days.)

3 Bring the stew to room temperature about an hour before baking. Make the dumplings by scalding the milk, nutmeg, and ½ teaspoon salt. Stir vigorously with a whisk while sprinkling in the semolina.

After all the semolina has been added, continue to whisk until the mixture is very thick and the foam subsides, about 1 minute. Turn off the heat and continue to whisk for 10 seconds to let off some of the heat.

4   Whisk a few tablespoons of the hot semolina into the yolks in a small bowl. Quickly whisk the egg mixture into the pot of semolina; add 1 tablespoon of the butter and ½ cup of the cheese and stir until well incorporated. Working quickly, spread the semolina mixture onto a nonstick jelly roll pan. The semolina should be just under ½ inch thick. Cool completely, about 45 minutes. The gnocchi can be refrigerated for up to two days at this point.

5   When ready to finish, preheat the oven to 375°F and position a rack in the middle of the oven. Place the lamb stew in a shallow 2-quart baking dish. Using a 2½-inch round cookie cutter, cut the semolina dough into circles. Starting from the outside, arrange the gnocchi in slightly overlapping concentric circles until you reach the center of the dish. Melt the remaining 1 tablespoon of butter and gently brush the top of the gnocchi with it; sprinkle with the remaining ½ cup cheese. Place the baking dish on a baking sheet, transfer to the oven, and bake until the top is brown and the stew is bubbling, 45 minutes to 1 hour.

>   To speed up browning the meat, use a second pan so you can cook two batches at once. Just make sure to deglaze the second pan with some of the wine or water in the recipe and add it to the stew.

>   If you don't have a biscuit or cookie cutter, use a juice glass. Dip it in water every few cuts to keep it from sticking.

SEMOLINA   Semolina, a pale creamy yellow flour ground from hard durum wheat, is the same flour that most extruded dried pasta is made from. Its delicate flavor and texture are ideal for making gnocchi and pizza. Look for it in Italian specialty stores

BAKED GROUPER WITH BLOOD ORANGES

SERVES 4

Four 8-ounce grouper fillets

2 blood or navel oranges

Coarse sea salt and freshly ground black
　　pepper

1 tablespoon plus 2 teaspoons olive oil

½ cup dry white wine

½ cup loosely packed chervil leaves

2 tablespoons thinly sliced chives or scallion
　　greens

This is an easy and fast way to cook any kind of fish fillets such as red snapper or striped bass. Try mint, parsley, cilantro, chives, or any combination of them in place of the chervil. Serve over fragrant basmati or jasmine rice.

1　Preheat the oven to 400°F. Place the fish, skin side down, in a glass or ceramic baking dish. Finely grate the orange zest over the fish and season with salt and pepper. Drizzle with 2 teaspoons oil and, using your hands, rub the zest, oil, salt, and pepper into the fish. Let the fish sit for 10 minutes.

2　Meanwhile, section the oranges. With a sharp knife, cut off the ends. Place each orange cut end down and slice off peel from top to bottom as close to the flesh as possible, making sure to remove all the white portion or pith. Holding the orange over a bowl so that you catch any juice, use a small paring knife to slice in between the membranes. Gently lift out the orange sections. Continue working all the way around the orange. Pour any juice over the fish along with the wine. Reserve the orange sections.

3　Coarsely chop the chervil and sprinkle half of it equally over the fillets. Set the other half aside. Transfer to the oven and bake for 20 minutes, or until the fish is opaque.

4　Meanwhile, mix the orange sections with the remaining 1 tablespoon oil, the remaining chervil, and the chives. When the fish is done, spoon the oranges over the fish and serve immediately.

CARAMELIZED ONION AND BACON TART

SERVES 6 TO 8

4 slices bacon, cut into ½-inch pieces

4 small onions, cut in half lengthwise and
thickly sliced

1 tablespoon plus 1 teaspoon thyme leaves,
chopped

Kosher salt

1 cup ricotta

1 large egg yolk

Pinch of freshly ground black pepper

¼ cup plus 1 tablespoon freshly grated
Parmigiano-Reggiano

1 blind-baked 8-inch tart shell
(see step 5, on page 34)

How can something so lowly and so ordinary as the poor onion become so luxurious and so rich? The secret to caramelized onions is long and slow cooking. Here, they are added to a wintry tart that can be served in small wedges as finger food, or in larger slices for a first course with a salad. For a more rustic look, or if you don't have a tart pan, follow the shaping and baking instructions for the Roasted Tomato Tart (page 172) instead of using the blind-baked shell called for below. (See photograph on page 148.)

1   Preheat the oven to 350°F. Cook the bacon in a medium frying pan over medium-high heat until the fat is mostly rendered and the bacon is crisp around the edges. Don't cook it too much now as it will be cooking again on top of the tart. Transfer to paper towels to drain and set aside, leaving 1 tablespoon of the bacon fat in the pan.

2   Add the onions to the pan and cook over medium-high heat until they start to brown, about 8 minutes. Turn the heat to medium-low and add 1 tablespoon of the thyme and a pinch of salt. Continue to cook until the onions are meltingly soft and deep golden brown, about 20 minutes more.

3   Meanwhile, combine the ricotta, egg yolk, ½ teaspoon salt, the pepper, the remaining 1 teaspoon thyme, and ¼ cup of the Parmigiano in a small bowl. Stir well to combine.

4   Spread the ricotta mixture evenly on the bottom of the tart shell. Arrange the onions on top of the ricotta and sprinkle with the remaining 1 tablespoon Parmigiano. Sprinkle the bacon over the top. Transfer to the oven and bake until the edges of the filling are golden brown, 30 to 40 minutes. Serve warm or at room temperature.

>   The small yellow onions that come in net bags at the supermarket are just the right size for this.

SERVES 6 TO 8

¾ cup ricotta

¼ cup freshly grated Parmigiano-Reggiano, plus more for rolling dough and sprinkling

½ teaspoon kosher salt

Freshly ground black pepper

2 large egg yolks

Handful of chopped fresh herbs such as oregano, thyme, or chives

½ recipe Tart Dough, prepared through step 2 and chilled (page 33)

10 to 15 Slow-Roasted Tomatoes (page 24)

2 teaspoons heavy cream or milk

Most of the tomatoes' moisture evaporates when they are slow-roasted, concentrating their flavor and making them ideal for using in a tart filling. Since the size of tomatoes varies so much, use your judgment as to how many will be necessary.

1 | Combine the ricotta, ¼ cup Parmigiano, salt, pepper, 1 egg yolk, and the herbs in a small bowl. Stir until well combined. Set aside.

2 | Dust a work surface with grated Parmigiano. Sprinkle more cheese on top of the dough. Roll into a rough circle about 10 inches in diameter and ⅛ inch thick. Turn frequently and dust with more cheese as needed to prevent sticking. Transfer to a baking sheet lined with parchment.

3 | Spread the filling on the dough, leaving about a 1½-inch border. Arrange the tomatoes on top, leaving a little space between them, and gently fold the edges of the dough toward the center, creating a 1- to 1½-inch border. Chill until firm.

4 | Preheat the oven to 425°F, and position the rack in the middle of the oven.

5 | Gently but firmly press the sides of the tart down with slightly cupped hands. This will prevent the tart from unfurling while baking. In a small bowl, whisk together the remaining egg yolk and the heavy cream. Brush the edges of the tart with the egg wash and then sprinkle with grated Parmigiano. Immediately transfer to the oven.

6 | After 10 minutes, reduce the oven temperature to 400°F, rotate the baking pan, and bake 20 minutes longer. The edges and bottom should be golden brown. Remove from the oven and slide the tart, on the parchment paper, onto a cooling rack. Serve warm or at room temperature.

SIMMER &

BRAISE

SINCE SIMMERING IS SUCH AN IMPORTANT PART OF BRAISING, THE SIMMERED AND BRAISED

recipes are together. Simmered dishes, mostly stocks and soups, are cooked completely on top of the stove over low heat. Braised meat dishes, on the other hand, involve thorough browning on top of the stove, followed by gentle simmering in liquid either on top of the stove or in the oven. If you are braising fish or vegetables, it's the same idea, but the cooking time is much shorter. Braised dishes such as lamb shanks or osso buco are a host's best friend because of their make-ahead and hard-to-overcook qualities.

When simmering, keep the heat low, or else the ingredients will cook too quickly and fall apart. There is a big difference between boiling and simmering, and even the best stoves need to be adjusted frequently to maintain a simmer. A good Dutch oven or braising pot made of enameled cast iron will keep braised dishes simmering gently in the oven by surrounding them with even, steady heat. Something about the word simmering is quieting in

and of itself. Perhaps I'm remembering my father telling us wild kids to "simmer down." It meant to get a hold of ourselves, relax, and turn down the heat.

Simmering isn't just a means to an end. You might think, "Well, if simmering is good, then boiling must be better. It's quicker," but that's wrong. It allows each vegetable in a *Soupe au Pistou* to retain its firm texture and individual character while lending some of its flavor to the broth and to the other vegetables in the soup. It also allows the fat and connective tissue of less-than-tender cuts of meat such as veal shanks to melt away slowly, moisturizing the meat, making it tender, and creating a rich sauce.

Braising is my favorite cooking technique during the cold, dark winter days. The basics of braising are: Take a tough cut of meat (often on the bone), brown it very well, cover it with liquid and let it cook, covered, very slowly in the oven or on top of the stove.

The resulting dish is the ultimate in winter comfort food. Don't turn up your nose at the term "tough cuts"—the very thing that makes them too tough for grilling or roasting makes them perfect for long, slow braising. The collagen and the connective tissue break down while cooking, melting into the sauce and giving it incomparable body and flavor.

You can serve a braised osso buco or lamb shank the same night you prepare it, but the real beauty of this method is you can prepare it a day or two ahead, and they will actually improve by sitting over that time. I've included stews here, since the method is virtually the same regardless of the size of the pieces of meat, and the fact that the meat for stews is boneless.

Precise timing is not as crucial in braising as it is in roasting or grilling. It is a very forgiving method, but if you are making a stew or braise ahead of time, err a little on the side of undercooking,

since it will be reheated later. You will have more control this way. Reheat in the oven or on top of the stove over low heat. The main pitfall of reheating is passing that "so tender it's falling from the bone" stage to the "it's falling apart completely" stage.

The two important things to remember when braising are brown enough and reduce enough. The same principles that apply to roasting apply to the browning stage of braising. Leave plenty of room so the food doesn't steam, and cook in batches so you are never browning more than a single layer at a time. Invest in a good Dutch oven or braising pot, one with a tight-fitting lid and a fairly large surface area so there's plenty of room to do your browning. Save time in the browning stage by using an additional large sauté pan, so you can do all the browning at one time, rather than in consecutive batches. Be sure to deglaze the extra pan with some of the liquid called for to capture every bit of flavor.

MAKES ABOUT 4 QUARTS

1 whole chicken (about 3½ pounds)

2 medium onions, unpeeled and halved

1 or 2 leeks, white part only, optional

2 celery stalks, cut into thirds

Small handful of celery leaves

2 or 3 parsnips, optional

3 small or 2 large carrots, scrubbed
　　and cut into 4-inch pieces

2 mushrooms, or leftover mushroom
　　stems, optional

Handful of flat-leaf parsley stems

A few thyme sprigs

1 scant teaspoon black peppercorns

1 bay leaf

1 teaspoon kosher salt, plus more
　　to season chicken

If I go to the trouble of making homemade stock—and I do because it is well worth the effort—I want to get some poached chicken for salads and sandwiches out of the deal. That's why I always start with a whole chicken rather than necks and backs, as some people do. Use the cooked chicken meat in chicken salad for lunch, or add it to a pan of sautéed vegetables to go over pasta or rice for a quick dinner.

1　Wash the chicken and place in a large stockpot. Add all remaining ingredients and fill with enough cold water to cover by 2 inches. Bring to a boil over high heat then reduce to a bare simmer. Simmer for 1 hour, skimming off the foam that rises to the top.

2　Remove the chicken by placing a large spoon in the cavity and carefully lifting it up. Drain any liquid over the pot before transferring the chicken to a plate. Let the chicken cool slightly, then carve off all white and dark meat, holding the chicken in place with a fork. Salt the chicken meat, cool slightly, cover, and refrigerate. Return the carcass and bones, along with any juices that accumulated on the plate, to the stockpot. Continue to simmer the stock for at least 1 hour more.

3　Strain the stock through a colander into a large bowl, and discard the solids. Strain again through a fine mesh sieve (lined with cheesecloth or a coffee filter if you have it) into another large bowl. Divide into small containers and let cool, then refrigerate until cold. Remove and discard the fat from the top, and freeze if not using right away. (If using immediately, skim off the fat using a wide flat spoon or use a fat separator.) Refrigerate for up to 4 days or freeze for up to 6 months.

> To make a clear, golden-hued stock, follow these simple guidelines:
>
> • Use as many yellow onion skins as you have around, and don't bother peeling the ones for the stock. Their natural color will help tint the stock.
>
> • Avoid anything that's dark green, like parsley leaves (stems are okay) and the dark green tops of leeks. These will contribute to turning the stock a murky color.
>
> • Stock should be simmered over the lowest possible flame; you may not even see a bubble, only steam.
>
> • Resist the urge to stir the stock and break up the bones; the less you touch it, the clearer it will be.

MAKES ABOUT 2 QUARTS

Kosher salt

8 to 10 pounds veal bones

2 medium onions, quartered

2 large carrots, cut into 2-inch pieces

2 celery stalks, cut into 2-inch pieces

6 garlic cloves, slightly crushed

3 tablespoons tomato paste

4 bay leaves, crumbled

2 or 3 thyme sprigs

1 teaspoon black peppercorns

This is a good project for a rainy or snowy day or a Sunday when you plan to be around the house all day. Buy the bones from your butcher and freeze them until you have time to make it, saving them, literally, for a rainy day. Making stock doesn't take a lot of work, just an occasional peek to make sure that it's cooking at a simmer. Once the stock is done, freeze it in handy amounts. Certain dishes are greatly enhanced by using a good homemade veal stock, such as Osso Buco (page 202) or Roast Fillet of Beef with Mushroom Sauce (page 138). You can also whip up a really great pan sauce anytime with some of this stock on hand. Just a little bit adds richness and body. I promise you, your cooking will be better.

1   Preheat the oven to 450°F. Lightly salt the bones and arrange them in a large roasting pan in a single layer. Cook until well browned on both sides, about 1 to 1½ hours, turning halfway through. Carefully pour off the accumulated fat. Add the onions, carrots, celery, and garlic. Plop the tomato paste on top of the bones, and roast for another 30 to 40 minutes.

2   Transfer the bones and vegetables to a large stockpot (at least 8 quarts), using tongs. Pour off the fat from the roasting pan and place it over 2 burners on your stove; turn on the heat to medium. Add 2 cups of water. Gently loosen the brown bits from the pan with a wooden spoon. When all the brown bits have been loosened, transfer the liquid to the stockpot and add another 3 quarts of water, or enough to cover the bones completely. Add the bay leaves, thyme, and peppercorns and bring to a simmer.

3   Skim any foam that rises to the surface, and cook over the lowest simmer possible for 4 to 6 hours, longer if possible. Let cool slightly, then strain the stock through a colander into a large bowl, discarding the solids. Strain again through a fine mesh sieve (lined with cheesecloth or a coffee filter if you have it) into another large bowl. Cool completely, then chill.

4   After it's chilled, remove the fat from the top. At this point, the stock can be returned to a saucepan and reduced by half for demi-glace, or it can be divided into small containers and refrigerated for up to 4 days or frozen for up to 6 months.

SERVES 4 TO 6

½ cup pearled barley

Kosher salt

2 large leeks (white and light green parts
   only)

1 tablespoon olive oil

¼ large fennel bulb, coarsely chopped
   (about 1 cup)

Freshly ground black pepper

1 bunch carrots, cut into ¼-inch circles
   (about 2 cups)

5 cups Golden Chicken Stock (page 178)

Poached chicken from the stock, torn into
   large chunks (see page 178)

½ teaspoon thyme leaves, optional

½ cup mixed chopped fresh herbs, such as
   parsley and dill

*Once you have made a batch of Golden Chicken Stock (page 178) and set aside the
meat, you can put this together in minutes. For a more concentrated chicken-y flavor,
simmer the stock until it tastes very rich before measuring out the five cups needed for
the recipe.*

1   Toast the barley by placing it in a small saucepan over medium-high
heat, swirling and stirring occasionally, until golden brown, about 15
minutes. Add 1½ cups cold water and ¼ teaspoon salt, and bring to a
boil. Once boiling, reduce to a steady simmer and cook until the barley
has reached the desired tenderness, about 30 minutes for a slightly
chewy texture. Drain and rinse under cool water to stop the cooking
and get rid of excess starch.

2   Slice the leeks in half lengthwise and then into ¼-inch slices. Transfer
to a large bowl of cold water and let soak for a few minutes so any resid-
ual sand or dirt sinks to the bottom of the bowl. Using a slotted spoon,
scoop out the leeks. If the leeks are very dirty, repeat the process with
a fresh bowl of water.

3   Heat the oil in a large saucepan. Add the leeks and fennel and sweat
over medium-low heat, 8 to 10 minutes. Season with salt and pepper.
Increase the heat to high and add the carrots and stock. Bring to a boil,
then reduce to a simmer and cook until the carrots are tender, about
20 minutes. Add the poached chicken, barley, and thyme, if using. Cook
until the chicken is hot. Adjust the salt and pepper to taste. Serve in
individual bowls garnished with freshly chopped herbs.

CHICKEN
STOCK

I do make and freeze my own chicken stock when I have the time, but there are times when
I run out and use store-bought stock. I prefer the brands that come in paper cartons, since
they don't have a metallic taste, like canned ones do. I also prefer low-sodium stocks so
they interfere minimally with the seasoning of the dish they're used in. Taste different
brands to find one you like.

SOUPE AU PISTOU

MAKES ABOUT 4 QUARTS

2 tablespoons olive oil

4 carrots: 1 minced, 3 thinly sliced

½ large or 1 small red onion, minced

2 celery stalks: 1 minced, 1 thinly sliced

2 red potatoes, cut into ½-inch cubes

2 leeks, cut in half lengthwise and thinly
    sliced and washed

3 cups finely shredded savoy cabbage

1 turnip, cubed (about 1½ cups)

1 cup fresh or canned chopped tomatoes

Kosher salt and freshly ground black pepper

1 bay leaf

6 to 8 cups Golden Chicken Stock
    (page 178)

2 cups haricots verts or green beans, cut
    into ¾-inch pieces

1 zucchini, cut into ½-inch cubes

2 cups Basic Cranberry Beans with 2 cups
    liquid (page 30) or 1 (15.5-ounces) can
    small white beans, drained and rinsed

1 cup fresh or frozen peas

1 teaspoon thyme leaves

Pistou (recipe follows)

Freshly grated Parmigiano-Reggiano

This French version of minestrone is the ultimate vegetable soup—packed with flavor and textures. It is adaptable to the season and to what you have on hand. The final swirl of brightly flavored pesto, or pistou, as it is called in France, brightens the soup's flavor and color.

1 In a large stockpot, heat the oil over medium heat. Add the minced carrots, minced onion, and minced celery. Sauté until golden brown, stirring frequently, 10 to 15 minutes. Add the remaining carrots and celery, the potatoes, leeks, cabbage, turnips, and tomatoes. Sauté over high heat until the cabbage wilts, about 5 minutes. Season with 1 teaspoon salt, and pepper to taste. Add the bay leaf and stock. (If using Basic Cranberry Beans, use only 6 cups of stock.) Bring to a boil and simmer until the potatoes are tender, stirring occasionally, about 25 minutes.

2 Add the haricots verts, zucchini, beans, peas, and thyme and continue to simmer until the green beans and zucchini are bright green and still crisp, about 10 minutes. Ladle into warm bowls and serve with the *pistou* and cheese on the side.

> **If you want to make the soup ahead of time, wait until reheating it to add the vegetables in step 2, so they stay green and crisp.**

MAKES ABOUT 2 CUPS

4 cups packed basil leaves

6 garlic cloves

1 teaspoon kosher salt

1 cup extra virgin olive oil

1 cup freshly grated Parmigiano-Reggiano

PISTOU

The French version of pesto is made without nuts. It will keep well for a few days in the refrigerator, providing you smooth the surface and cover with a thin layer of olive oil. To preserve its color, store it in a deep container with a minimum of surface area, like a small jar.

In a mini food processor or blender, coarsely chop the basil, garlic, and salt. Slowly drizzle in the oil and blend until smooth. Add the cheese and pulse to blend.

PUREED VEGETABLE SOUPS

- Just about any vegetable can be used to make a pureed soup. The goal is to highlight a single flavor such as corn, mushroom, pea, or winter squash. Other vegetables good for purees are potato, asparagus, tomato, summer squash, fava bean, carrot, fennel, and broccoli.

- Start by sweating aromatic vegetables—at the very least, some kind of onion, whether it is shallot, leek, or onion. Depending on the final flavor and color of the soup, you may also want to use garlic, carrot, or celery, but just enough to complement the main ingredient, not overwhelm it. For instance, carrots added to a tomato puree impart a sweetness that balances the acidity of the tomatoes. Carrots in a mushroom soup would muddle the flavors and the color. Add the main ingredient and a small amount of potato if it is a watery (mushrooms), rather than a starchy (squash, peas) vegetable.

- Next add the main vegetable and cook it for a few minutes. Add just enough liquid to cover the vegetables. If using a watery vegetable, like mushrooms, cook them until they have lost their volume to better gauge the amount of liquid needed. You can always thin a soup later, but it's harder to thicken it once finished. Also take into account that you may be adding cream or milk at the end to finish the soup.

- Whether or not to strain the puree before the final step of finishing it is up to you. Some soups, like mushroom, are good with a little texture, but the end result will be more refined if you take the extra step of passing it through a fine sieve. There's no need to strain butternut squash soup, which becomes smooth when pureed in a blender.

- You can use a bar blender or an immersion blender (see page 13) to puree the soup. To use a bar blender, make sure the soup has cooled a bit before you puree it, and never fill the blender jar more than halfway. Leave the center cap of the lid slightly ajar to allow steam to escape. Just to be safe, place a dishtowel loosely over the top of the blender to catch any spills. These steps will prevent the soup from overflowing the blender. An immersion blender can be used directly in the pot you cooked the vegetables in; while it may not produce as smooth a puree, it is certainly convenient. Make sure to keep the blade of the blender submerged to avoid spattering. I don't recommend using food processors for this job, as they tend to leak.

- If making a pureed soup ahead of time, prepare the base or basic puree, and refrigerate or freeze. When ready to serve, reheat, thin as needed with stock, milk, or cream, and add the final seasonings such as herbs, cheese, salt, and pepper. Like chunky soups, the flavors will improve as they sit, except for something like pea or asparagus soup, which are better served right away to preserve their delicate colors and flavors.

CLOCKWISE FROM TOP RIGHT: WILD MUSHROOM BISQUE, SWEET CORN PUREE, BUTTERNUT SQUASH BISQUE, AND GREEN PEA PUREE

SERVES 4 TO 6

1 cup dried porcini mushrooms

2 pounds mixed mushrooms such as
cremini, button, and shiitake

1 tablespoon olive oil

1 tablespoon unsalted butter

4 shallots, thinly sliced

Kosher salt and freshly ground black pepper

1 teaspoon rosemary leaves

1 celery stalk, thinly sliced

¼ cup plus 2 tablespoons Madeira or
sweet sherry

1 medium Yukon gold potato, peeled and cut
into 2-inch cubes

1 cup Golden Chicken Stock (page 178)

1 teaspoon thyme or tarragon leaves,
chopped

1 cup milk or heavy cream

Even if you use only fresh cultivated button mushrooms in this soup, the dried porcini will provide a woodsy wild mushroom flavor. Garnish with additional sautéed mushrooms and chives or tarragon.

1   Bring 2 cups of water to boil. Place porcini mushrooms in a large heat-proof glass measuring cup. Pour water over mushrooms and set aside. Clean and trim the fresh mushrooms. Cut into quarters and set aside.

2   Heat the oil and butter in a large stockpot over medium heat. Add the shallots, a pinch of salt and pepper, and rosemary. Cook over medium heat, stirring occasionally, until the shallots begin to brown, about 7 minutes. Add the celery and cook until translucent, about 2 minutes. Add the fresh mushrooms and generously season with salt and pepper, stirring frequently for about 5 minutes, until the mushrooms lose about half their volume.

3   Remove the porcini mushrooms from the water using a slotted spoon and add them to the stockpot. Increase the heat to medium-high and add ¼ cup Madeira. Cook for 1 minute.

4   Slowly pour the porcini liquid into the stockpot leaving behind any sand. Add the potato and stock and bring to a boil, then reduce to a simmer and cook until the potato is tender, about 20 minutes. Turn off the heat and let the soup cool slightly, stirring to let off heat.

5   Puree the soup using a bar blender or immersion blender. If using a bar blender, fill the jar no more than halfway and blend until smooth. Transfer to a clean pot or storage container. Continue until all of the soup is pureed. If using an immersion blender, puree thoroughly right in the pot it was cooked in. (At this point the soup can be refrigerated for up to 2 days or frozen for up to 2 months.)

6   When ready to serve, reheat the soup in a clean pot. Add the thyme and milk and stir well. If necessary, thin to desired thickness by adding additional milk, cream, or stock. Simmer for 5 minutes. Adjust seasoning. Turn off heat, add the remaining 2 tablespoons Madeira, stir well, and serve immediately.

SWEET CORN PUREE

SERVES 4 TO 6

1 leek (white and light green parts only)

4 ears yellow or white corn, or 2 to 3 cups frozen kernels

1 tablespoon unsalted butter

Kosher salt

1 medium Yukon gold potato, cut into 1-inch pieces

1 bay leaf

A few thyme sprigs

4 cups Golden Chicken Stock (page 178)

¼ cup milk or heavy cream

If using canned chicken stock, purchase one that is light in color. Some of them are quite brown, which will throw off the color of this soup. Garnish the soup with leftover shredded chicken, diced jalapeño, and scallions or chives. Try a bit of sour cream or crème fraîche and jalapeño, or, of course, some cooked corn.

1   Slice the leek in half lengthwise and then into ¼-inch slices. Transfer to a large bowl of cold water and let soak for a few minutes to let the sand sink to the bottom of the bowl. Using a slotted spoon, scoop out the leek, place in a sieve and give it a good rinse. If the leek is very dirty repeat the process with a fresh bowl of water. Set aside. Cut the corn off the cobs, and discard the cobs (see page 57).

2   Heat the butter in a large stockpot over medium heat. Add the leek and a pinch of salt and cook over low heat, stirring occasionally, until the leek is translucent but has not yet begun to brown, about 5 minutes. Add the potato, corn, bay leaf, thyme, and chicken stock.

3   Bring to a boil, then reduce to a simmer. Cook until the potato is tender, about 15 minutes. Turn off the heat and let the soup cool slightly. Remove and discard the bay leaf.

4   Puree the soup using a bar blender or immersion blender. If using a bar blender, fill the jar no more than halfway and blend until smooth. Transfer to a clean pot or storage container. Continue until all of the soup is pureed. If using an immersion blender, puree thoroughly right in the pot it was cooked in. (At this point the soup can be refrigerated for up to 2 days or frozen for up to 2 months.)

5   When ready to serve, reheat the soup in a clean pot. Add the milk and stir well. If necessary, thin to desired thickness by adding additional milk, cream, or stock. Simmer for 5 minutes. Adjust seasoning and serve immediately.

BUTTERNUT SQUASH BISQUE

SERVES 4 TO 6

1 medium butternut squash, about 2 pounds

1 tablespoon olive oil

1 medium yellow onion, cut in half and thinly
   sliced

1 celery stalk, thinly sliced

1 carrot, thinly sliced

1 teaspoon rosemary leaves

Kosher salt and freshly ground black pepper

2 cups Golden Chicken Stock (page 178),
   or vegetable stock

¾ cup milk or cream

Adding that leftover Parmesan rind that's been lurking in the back of the refrigerator to the soup while it is simmering in step 3 will add a subtle cheese flavor. Be sure to remove it before serving. Or, add the rind at the end of step 5, while keeping the soup warm until serving, along with another sprig of rosemary. Both will infuse the soup with a final burst of flavor. Again, remove them before serving. Garnish with toasted pepitas and a drizzle of pumpkin seed oil (see page 126).

1   Peel the squash, cut open, and remove the seeds. Cut into 2-inch chunks and set aside.

2   Add the oil to a stockpot and place over medium heat. Add the onion, celery, carrot, rosemary, and a pinch of salt and pepper, and cook until the onion begins to brown, about 15 minutes.

3   Add the squash, stock, and 1 cup water. Bring to a boil, then reduce to a simmer and cook until the squash is tender, about 15 minutes. Turn off the heat and let the soup cool slightly.

4   Puree the soup using a bar blender or immersion blender. If using a bar blender, fill the jar no more than halfway and blend until smooth. Transfer to a clean pot or storage container. Continue until all of the soup is pureed. If using an immersion blender, puree thoroughly right in the pot it was cooked in. (At this point the soup can be refrigerated for up to 2 days or frozen for up to 2 months.)

5   When ready to serve, reheat the soup in a clean pot. Add the milk and stir well. If necessary, thin to desired thickness by adding additional milk, cream, or stock. Simmer for 5 minutes. Keep warm until ready to serve. Adjust seasoning and serve immediately.

GREEN PEA PUREE

SERVES 4 TO 6

3 medium leeks (white and light green parts
   only)

3 tablespoons unsalted butter

2 shallots, thinly sliced

2 garlic cloves, chopped

Kosher salt and freshly ground black pepper

3 tablespoons fresh herbs such as tarragon,
   chervil, or thyme

4 cups fresh (4 pounds unshelled) or frozen
   peas, thawed if frozen

3 cups Golden Chicken Stock (page 178)

½ cup heavy cream or milk, optional

Use a light-colored chicken stock here to prevent the soup from turning murky. Delicate herbs such as tarragon, chervil, or soft thyme are good partners. Consider garnishes of sugar snap peas, pea shoots, or cooked diced bacon.

1   Slice the leeks in half lengthwise and then into ¼-inch slices. Transfer to a large bowl of cold water and let soak for a few minutes to let the sand sink to the bottom of the bowl. Using a slotted spoon, scoop out the leeks, place in a sieve, and give them a good rinse. If the leeks are very dirty, repeat the process with a fresh bowl of water. Set aside.

2   Heat the butter in a large stockpot over medium heat. Add the leeks, shallots, garlic, and a large pinch of salt and pepper. Cook, stirring occasionally, until the vegetables are translucent, about 10 minutes. Add 2 tablespoons of the fresh herbs and cook for 30 seconds.

3   Add the peas and stock and bring to a boil, then reduce to a simmer and cook for 10 minutes. Turn off the heat and let the soup cool slightly.

4   Puree the soup using a bar blender or immersion blender. If using a bar blender, fill the jar no more than halfway and blend until smooth. Add the remaining tablespoon of herbs in the last batch. Transfer to a clean pot or storage container. Continue until all of the soup is pureed. If using an immersion blender, add the remaining tablespoon of herbs and puree thoroughly right in the pot it was cooked in. (At this point the soup can be refrigerated for up to 1 day.)

5   When ready to serve, reheat the soup in a clean pot. Add the cream, if using, and stir well. If necessary, thin to desired thickness by adding additional milk, cream, or stock. Simmer for 5 minutes. Adjust seasoning and serve immediately.

SERVES 4

2 stalks lemongrass

4 large ears sweet corn

2 teaspoons green curry paste

1 can (13½ ounces) regular coconut milk

1 can (13½ ounces) light coconut milk

2 tablespoons Asian or Thai fish sauce
    (see below)

1 teaspoon kosher salt

2 teaspoons sugar

24 littleneck clams (about 2 pounds), well
    scrubbed

12 mussels (about ½ pound), well scrubbed

16 large shrimp (about ½ pound), peeled
    and deveined

1 pound striped bass, or other meaty white
    fish, such as halibut or grouper, cut into
    4 equal-size chunks

12 small basil leaves, torn

1 fresh red chile, thinly sliced, optional

Cooked jasmine rice

2 limes, cut into wedges

In this Asian stew with a New England sensibility, sweet fresh corn is a natural with the spicy coconut milk–based broth. It is unbelievably easy and fast to make. It's a great dinner party dish, but if you want to double the recipe, it is easier to make in two pots rather than one large one to give the clams and mussels plenty of room to open. Serve over jasmine rice, preceded by Thai Cole Slaw (page 53).

1 | Prepare the lemongrass by peeling the 2 or 3 outer layers of the stalk. Cut off the fibrous tops about 3 to 4 inches from the bases and discard, using only the bottom bulbs. Using the flat side of a large knife and the heel of your hand, smash the lemongrass. Set aside. Husk the corn and cut off the kernels by standing the ears on end and cutting straight down into a large bowl (see page 57).

2 | Place the green curry paste in a large wok or large saucepan and whisk in 1 can coconut milk. Cook over medium heat for 2 to 3 minutes. Whisk in the remaining can coconut milk, the fish sauce, salt, and sugar. Add the lemongrass and corn, then cover and simmer for 5 minutes.

3 | Add the clams and mussels. Cover and continue to simmer 10 to 12 minutes, until the shells are at least halfway open. Discard any clams or mussels that don't open. Add the shrimp and fish, making sure the fish is submerged in the broth. If necessary, move the clams and mussels to the side of the pan. Cover and continue to simmer 6 to 8 minutes, until the fish is opaque. Turn off the heat and let sit for 2 to 3 minutes, covered. Sprinkle with the basil and chile, if using. Serve over jasmine rice with wedges of lime.

GREEN CURRY PASTE

Available in small jars or larger plastic tubs, green curry paste is a blend of many herbs and spices. Combined with coconut milk, it makes a delicious broth which can be used as a base for soups and stews. It is very spicy, and a little goes a long way.

FISH SAUCE

This ubiquitous salty seasoning of Southeast Asia, made from fermented fish, gives that unmistakably authentic flavor to Thai and Vietnamese dishes. Once opened, it keeps for a very long time. Vietnamese fish sauce is called *nuoc nam*, Thai fish sauce is called *nam pla*.

SERVES 6

4 large russet (baking) potatoes (about 2½
pounds), scrubbed

1 teaspoon kosher salt

1 cup loosely packed mint or basil leaves

1 cup hot milk

2 tablespoons unsalted butter, room
temperature

Coarse sea salt and freshly ground
black pepper

These potatoes are infused with the color and flavor of mint. If you use a food mill to puree the potatoes, add the blanched mint to the mill, which will result in potatoes that are flecked with green, rather than tinted. If mashing by hand or using a ricer, puree the mint with the milk as in step 3. Basil can be substituted. Serve with Herb-Crusted Lamb. (See photograph on page 106.)

1   Cut the potatoes in half crosswise. Place in a large pot and fill with enough cold water to cover the potatoes by a few inches. Add the kosher salt and bring to a boil. Simmer until tender (potatoes should be easily pierced with a paring knife), 15 to 20 minutes. Drain and set aside until cool enough to handle.

2   Meanwhile, bring a small saucepan of water to a boil and add the mint. Remove the mint as soon as it turns bright green, 5 to 10 seconds. Drain through a sieve and run under cold water until cool. Squeeze out excess water with your hand.

3   Combine the milk and mint in a blender and blend well.

4   Put the potatoes through a food mill or ricer, or mash them well using a fine potato masher, and place in the top of a double boiler. (If mashing, first slide off and discard the potato skins.) Combine the potatoes with the milk mixture, working over simmering water so the potatoes stay hot. Stir in the butter and season with sea salt and pepper to taste. Serve immediately.

>   If you don't have a double boiler, create one by setting a metal bowl over a saucepan. Choose a bowl that will fit at least halfway into the saucepan to keep the potatoes really hot. Cover with foil and keep the water simmering until ready to serve.

MAKES 18

1 pound fresh unshelled cranberry beans
   (about 1¾ cups shelled)

Extra virgin olive oil

4 garlic cloves: 2 whole, 2 cut in half

20 large sage leaves

¼ teaspoon kosher salt

⅛ teaspoon freshly ground black pepper

½ crusty baguette

Coarse sea salt

The key to this tasty hors d'oeuvre is to cook the beans to just the right consistency, so they hold their shape on top of the bread without sliding off. Should the beans start to dry out in the pan, add a little extra water; cook a little longer if they are too wet. The beans will thicken a little as they cool. (See photograph on page 194.)

1 | Shell the cranberry beans and rinse with cold water. Sauté the 2 whole garlic cloves in 1 tablespoon oil over medium-high heat in a small saucepan until golden brown all over, 5 to 10 minutes. Add 2 sage leaves and cook for 30 seconds. Add the beans and 2 cups cold water. Bring to a boil and then reduce to a steady simmer over medium-low heat, cooking until the beans are tender when pierced with a paring knife, stirring occasionally, about 35 minutes.

2 | Remove the sage from the beans and discard. Season with the kosher salt and the pepper. Using a fork, mash the garlic and about ¼ cup of the beans on the side of the pan. Thicken the mixture over high heat about 2 minutes, stirring frequently, until the liquid looks like a very thick soup. Transfer to a bowl and let cool, stirring occasionally. Add 1 to 2 tablespoons olive oil and stir well.

3 | Preheat the oven to 375°F. Heat a small frying pan and add about ¼ inch of oil. Heat until hot but not smoking. Test by dropping a sage leaf in the oil. It should sizzle and turn bright green. Add the remaining sage leaves a few at a time, transferring them to a paper towel as soon as they turn bright green, 20 to 25 seconds. Discard the oil.

4 | Slice the baguette into eighteen ¼- to ½-inch disks and place on a large baking sheet. Toast until golden brown, 10 to 12 minutes, turning halfway through to toast other side. Rub each slice lightly with a halved garlic clove. Spoon some of the beans onto each piece of bread. Drizzle with olive oil and garnish each with a fried sage leaf and a sprinkle of sea salt.

> When cooking beans, keep a kettle of water simmering on the stove. If you need to add water, add the hot water to keep the beans at a steady simmer.

CRANBERRY BEAN CROSTINI

SERVES 6 TO 8

½ pound slab bacon, cut into ¼- to ½-inch-
  thick slices

3 pounds beef chuck, cut into 2-inch cubes

Kosher salt and freshly ground black pepper

3 or 4 garlic cloves, thinly sliced

3 tablespoons all-purpose flour

1 teaspoon tomato paste

1 bottle dry red wine

2 cups low-sodium beef stock or Brown Veal
  Stock (page 179)

1 carrot, finely chopped

1 package (8 ounces) cipollini or white pearl
  onions, peeled, leaving root end intact

1 package (10 ounces) white mushrooms,
  trimmed and quartered

1 bouquet garni (see below)

Chopped flat-leaf parsley, for garnish

Everything old is new again. Every 1960's housewife knew how to make this classic stew, and then it went out of style in favor of trendier dishes, but it is still one of the best winter dinner party dishes around. It can be made several days ahead of time, and the side dishes are easy to make, too—one in the oven and one on the stove. Thyme-Roasted Carrots (page 141) and Potato-Celeriac Mash (page 198) complete the menu. Serve a crisp green salad before or after, and a dessert such as Caramel Apple Tart (page 225) to complete the French theme.

1 | Cut the bacon into ¼- to ½-inch squares. Place in a Dutch oven or large heavy pot, and cook over medium heat until browned and crisp, about 25 minutes. Remove the bacon with a slotted spoon, drain on paper towels, and set aside. Pour off all but 2 tablespoons of the fat in the pot.

2 | Season the beef with salt and pepper. Arrange the meat in a single layer and brown over high heat. (Browning may need to be done in 2 or more batches depending on the size of the pan.) Once all the meat has been browned, add the garlic and cook 2 to 3 minutes. Add the flour, stir well, and cook for about 5 minutes, until browned. Stir in the tomato paste and deglaze the pan by adding the wine, making sure to scrape up all the brown bits with a wooden spoon.

3 | Add the stock, carrot, onions, mushrooms, half of the browned bacon, 1 teaspoon salt, a pinch of pepper, and the bouquet garni. Bring to a boil, reduce to a simmer, and cover. After 1½ to 2 hours, once the meat begins to get tender, crack the lid an inch or two so the sauce can thicken. (Depending on the amount of liquid in the pan, the lid may be taken off completely.) Continue to cook for a total of 2½ to 3 hours, stirring occasionally, until the meat is very tender, and the sauce has thickened. Garnish with the remaining bacon and chopped parsley.

> **Drop pearl onions into boiling water for 30 seconds. The peels will slide right off.**

> **Freezing bacon for 15 minutes will make it easier to cut.**

> **If making ahead of time, cook 30 minutes less than the recipe states. That way, you can re-heat it without worrying about the meat falling apart. Reheat until it is perfectly fork tender.**

BOUQUET GARNI | A bunch of fresh or dried herbs—usually parsley, thyme, and bay leaf—that is tied together in a bundle or wrapped in cheesecloth and is used to flavor soups, stocks, and sauces. I like to buy ready-made ones, which look a bit like green cigars, with white string holding them together. These are widely available, but I like the ones from Oliviers & Co. (see Sources, page 254).

SERVES 6

4 russet (baking) potatoes, scrubbed

2 medium celeriac (celery root), peeled

Kosher salt

¾ cup hot milk

3 tablespoons unsalted butter

Freshly ground black pepper

Celeriac, also called celery root, may look a bit scary, but once you slice off the gnarly skin, a versatile, semi-starchy vegetable with a mild taste of celery is revealed. Look for those that are about the size of a large grapefruit and feel heavy for their size. They lighten the texture and add another dimension to mashed potatoes.

1 | Cut the potatoes in half and the celeriac into quarters. Place in a large pot and fill with cold water so that the potatoes and celeriac are covered by a few inches. Add 1 teaspoon salt and place a smaller pot lid on the vegetables to keep them submerged. Bring to a boil. Cook until tender (vegetables should be easily pierced with a paring knife), 15 to 20 minutes. Drain and return the vegetables to the hot pot to remove excess moisture.

2 | Put the potatoes and celeriac through a food mill or ricer, or mash them well using a fine potato masher. (If mashing, slide off and discard the potato skins.) Combine the vegetables with the milk and stir in the butter. Season with 1 teaspoon salt, or more to taste, and pepper. Serve immediately.

> To keep potatoes piping hot for serving, place them in a metal bowl over a large saucepan or stockpot of simmering water, and cover with foil. Stir occasionally. You may need to add more milk just before serving.

SHALLOTS | Shallots are a staple in my kitchen. They can vary greatly in size, yielding anywhere from 1 to 4 tablespoons when minced. They are sometimes separated into two large cloves; each clove should be counted as one shallot. They lend a sweet, delicate, oniony flavor to dishes that's never overpowering. Use them as you would garlic—a clove or two at a time to start a dish or pan sauce. They can be finely minced or thinly sliced into rings.

TAGINE-STYLE LAMB SHANKS

SERVES 4

Olive or vegetable oil

2 teaspoons ground cumin

2 teaspoons ground coriander

4 lamb shanks (1 pound each) trimmed of
    excess fat

Kosher salt and freshly ground black pepper

2 medium onions, halved lengthwise and
    thinly sliced

1 tablespoon tomato paste

2 pinches of red pepper flakes

1 cup dried fruit, such as pitted prunes
    and/or apricots

1 cinnamon stick

1 to 2 teaspoons freshly grated ginger

Lamb shanks are a tough cut of meat that benefit from a long, slow braise. Water can be used in place of stock, and the end result will still be a rich, thick, and flavorful sauce, thanks to the fruit, spices, and the meat itself. Like a Morrocan tagine, which is usually made with stewing meat, these shanks should be served over couscous.

1　Preheat the oven to 325°F. Coat the bottom of a Dutch oven or other large heavy pot with a tight-fitting lid with oil. Combine the cumin and coriander in a small bowl and mix well.

2　Season the lamb shanks generously with salt and pepper and coat evenly with the spice mixture. Transfer to the pot and brown well on all sides over medium-high heat, 20 to 25 minutes. If there is any sign of burning, reduce the heat to medium. Transfer to a plate and set aside.

3　Add the onions, tomato paste, and red pepper flakes to the pot and cook until the onions are transparent and soft, about 10 minutes. Return the shanks to the pot. Add the dried fruit, a pinch of salt, the cinnamon stick, ginger, and enough water to just cover the shanks. Bring to a simmer, then cover and transfer to the oven for 2 to 2½ hours, occasionally skimming the foam that rises to the top. The meat should be very tender and starting to fall from the bone. The dish can be made ahead of time up to this point. Refrigerate in a large airtight container or right in the pot. When ready to continue, remove any hardened fat that has collected on the surface and rewarm. If continuing with recipe, skim fat from surface with a spoon.

4　Remove the shanks and enough of the fruit with a slotted spoon to garnish each plate and set aside. Reduce the sauce by half over high heat on top of the stove, about 40 minutes. It should look like a thick gravy.

5　Lower the flame and return the shanks to the sauce along with any juices that have collected on the plate. Cook until hot, about 10 minutes. (Once the sauce is reduced, the shanks may also be reheated in the sauce by placing in a warm oven (about 250°F) where they can be kept until ready to serve.)

OSSO BUCO WITH TOASTED GARLIC GREMOLATA

SERVES 6

6 pieces veal shank (2½ to 3 inches thick, 1 pound each)

2 tablespoons olive oil

Kosher salt and freshly ground black pepper

All-purpose flour, for dredging

1 celery stalk, finely diced

1 carrot, finely diced

½ onion, finely diced

2 garlic cloves, very finely minced

½ cup dry Marsala

½ cup dry white wine

2 large thyme sprigs

1 tablespoon chopped flat-leaf parsley

1 bay leaf

1-inch piece orange peel, pith removed

1-inch piece lemon peel, pith removed

4 cups Brown Veal Stock (page 179)

1 cup canned whole tomatoes in juice

Risotto alla Milanese (page 205)

Toasted Garlic Gremolata (page 204)

Osso Buco, which means "bone with a hole" in Italian, is another braised dish that can be made one or two days ahead. It will only improve as it sits. If you don't have Brown Veal Stock (page 179) for this, then use good chicken stock and at least some store-bought demi-glace (see Sources) instead. Just remember to compensate for the salt that they may contain. Serve with Risotto alla Milanese (page 205) or Potato-Celeriac Mash (page 198).

1 Preheat the oven to 350°F. Tie a piece of butcher's twine around each shank if your butcher has not already done so.

2 Heat the oil in a sauté pan large enough to hold all 6 veal shank pieces. Season the veal with salt and pepper and dredge the cut sides (top and bottom) in flour, shaking off any excess. Place the shanks in the pan, in a single layer, pressing them firmly down so they make good contact with the pan. Once the shanks have browned, 8 to 10 minutes, turn them and brown the other side, pressing them down again. The second side should brown in 6 to 8 minutes.

3 Transfer the shanks to a Dutch oven or other heavy pot large enough to hold them in a single layer. You can also use a large roasting pan, and cover it tightly with foil. If they don't quite fit in a single layer, rearrange them several times during the braising time. Leave 2 tablespoons fat in the sauté pan; discard the rest.

4 Add the celery, carrot, onion, and garlic to the sauté pan and cook until soft, about 10 minutes. Add the Marsala and white wine, stirring with a wooden spoon to loosen and dissolve all the brown bits. Add the thyme, parsley, bay leaf, orange and lemon peels, 1 teaspoon salt, ½ teaspoon pepper, the stock, and tomatoes and bring to a boil.

5 Once the mixture boils, pour over the shanks and cover tightly with a lid or aluminum foil. Place in the oven and cook for 1 hour. After 1 hour, turn the shanks, cover again tightly, and continue to cook for about 1 hour more, until the meat begins to fall from the bone.

6 | Remove the shanks from the Dutch oven and set aside. Discard the orange and lemon peels. Place the Dutch oven on the stove. Reduce the sauce over medium-high heat until thick, about 40 minutes. Discard the bay leaf and sprigs of thyme. Return the shanks to the sauce to heat through. Plate the shanks, with the small end of the bone facing up, and spoon the sauce over them. Serve with the risotto and the gremolata.

> If making ahead of time, cook 30 minutes less than the recipe states. That way, you can reheat it when ready to serve without worrying about the meat falling apart. Reheat until perfectly fork tender.

TOASTED GARLIC GREMOLATA

SERVES 6

1 tablespoon extra virgin olive oil

2 garlic cloves or 1 shallot, very finely
   minced

Zest of 1 lemon, chopped

2 tablespoons finely chopped flat-leaf
   parsley

¼ teaspoon coarse sea salt

Gremolata, the garnish for osso buco, is traditionally made with raw garlic, lemon zest, and herbs, and adds a note of fresh, bright flavor to the rich dish. I find the taste of raw garlic a little overwhelming with it, so I toast the garlic until golden to soften its harshness.

1 | Heat a small sauté pan over very low heat and add the oil and the garlic. Cook gently until golden brown, 5 to 10 minutes. Immediately remove the garlic from the pan to prevent it from burning. Set aside in a small bowl and cool.

2 | Add the lemon zest, parsley, and salt to the toasted garlic and mix well. Place about ½ teaspoon on each piece of veal shank.

RISOTTO ALLA MILANESE

SERVES 6

About 6 cups Golden Chicken Stock
    (page 178)

1 teaspoon saffron threads, loosely packed

3 tablespoons unsalted butter

1 tablespoon olive oil

1 shallot, minced

2 cups Arborio rice

½ cup dry white wine

¼ cup freshly grated Parmigiano-Reggiano

Kosher salt and freshly ground black pepper

This bright yellow, saffron-infused rice is the traditional Italian partner for osso buco. It's one of the few instances when risotto should be served as a side dish rather than a primo, or first course. Make it when the osso buco reheats.

1   Bring the chicken stock to a boil in a large saucepan and reduce to a simmer (I like to keep the stock on the burner directly behind the one on which I'm making the risotto). Remove ½ cup of chicken stock, crumble in the saffron, and keep warm.

2   Heat 1 tablespoon of the butter and the oil in a medium shallow saucepan over medium heat. Add the shallot and cook until translucent, 5 to 7 minutes. Add the rice and stir well to coat the rice evenly. Continue to cook, stirring frequently, until the rice turns translucent on the edges, about 4 minutes.

3   Add the wine and stir until it is absorbed. Add the saffron-infused stock, and cook, stirring, until it has been nearly absorbed. Add the stock one ladle (about ½ cup) at a time, stirring continuously. Continue to add stock as each addition is absorbed. The idea is to keep the rice thinly veiled with stock at all times. It should evenly and gently bubble, not boil furiously. It should never be completely dry, and it should not be flooded with stock, either. It will absorb liquid more quickly toward the beginning of the cooking time than at the end.

4   You may not need to add all of the stock. The risotto should be a creamy porridge, and each grain should have a slight bite to it in the center, but not a crunch. Before adding the final ladle, turn the heat off. It will continue to thicken as you finish it and get it to the table, so it should be a touch looser than you want it when you take it off the heat. Total cooking time is between 18 and 20 minutes. Add the cheese and the remaining 2 tablespoons butter, and season with salt and pepper to taste.

> Technically, risotto needs to be stirred constantly, but I find I can get other things done nearby in the kitchen while it's cooking, so let's just say it needs to be stirred every few minutes.

PAPPARDELLE WITH OSSO BUCO RAGÙ

SERVES 2 AS A MAIN COURSE

1 cup dried porcini mushrooms

1 tablespoon olive oil

3 garlic cloves, chopped

1 tablespoon rosemary leaves, finely
  chopped

Pinch of red pepper flakes

Kosher salt and freshly ground black pepper

1 cup crushed tomatoes in juice

1 leftover osso buco with sauce, shredded
  off the bone (marrow optional)

½ pound pappardelle, tagliatelle, or
  spaghetti

Toasted Garlic Gremolata (page 204),
  optional

Freshly grated Parmigiano-Reggiano,
  optional

One leftover piece of veal shank. Two people. I make a ragù with some dried porcini and canned tomatoes from my pantry, and serve it with pasta. Dinner for two.

1   Bring 1 cup of water to a boil. Place the porcini mushrooms in a large heatproof glass measuring cup. Pour the water over the mushrooms and set aside.

2   Heat a large frying pan over low heat. Add the oil and sauté the garlic until golden brown, 5 to 8 minutes. Remove the mushrooms from the water using a slotted spoon and finely chop, reserving the soaking liquid. Add the rosemary, red pepper flakes, mushrooms, and a pinch of salt and pepper to the garlic and simmer over medium heat for about 5 minutes. Slowly pour the porcini liquid into the pan, leaving any sand behind. Cook until the mushroom liquid reduces by about half, 5 to 10 minutes.

3   Add the tomatoes and juice. Simmer for 5 minutes and then add the meat, marrow, if using, and any leftover osso buco sauce. Continue to simmer until thick, about 15 minutes.

4   While the sauce simmers, bring a large pot of water to a boil for the pasta. Add salt and the pasta to the water. Cook the pasta according to the package directions, stirring occasionally, until al dente. Drain the pasta and add it to the ragù. Gently stir so that the pasta is evenly coated with sauce. Serve with gremolata or top with cheese, if desired, and serve.

BRAISED ENDIVE

SERVES 4

4 heads Belgian endive, discolored outer
    leaves removed and bottoms trimmed

1 teaspoon sugar

1 tablespoon unsalted butter

Kosher salt and freshly ground black pepper

Juice of 1 orange

½ cup Golden Chicken Stock (page 178)

Belgian endive are grown in the dark to preserve their creamy whitish yellow color. Quickly braising them in chicken stock and orange juice transforms them into a silky side vegetable. (See photograph on page 128.)

1 | Slice each head of endive in half lengthwise and sprinkle the cut side evenly with the sugar. Melt the butter in a large sauté pan over medium-high heat until it foams. Place the endive cut side down in the pan. Place a smaller heavy pan on top of the endive to weigh them and press down so that there is good contact between the endive and the pan. Cook until the edges of the endive leaves turn golden brown, 2 to 3 minutes.

2 | Turn the endive over and season with salt and pepper. Pour the orange juice over the endive. Once the juice has been reduced to a glaze, 1 to 2 minutes, add the stock, increase heat to high, and bring to a boil. Cook until the stock has been reduced to a thick glaze and the endive are tender, about 5 minutes. If the endive are tender before the stock is reduced, remove the endive and continue to reduce the stock.

SPICY BRAISED BROCCOLI RABE

SERVES 4 AS A SIDE DISH

1 pound broccoli rabe

2 tablespoons extra virgin olive oil, plus
    more for drizzling

3 garlic cloves, cut in half

1 large pinch of red pepper flakes

Kosher salt

½ cup Golden Chicken Stock (page 178)

I love the natural bitterness of broccoli rabe, also called rapini, but you can soften it a bit by blanching it. Go easy on the red pepper flakes at first, you can always add more later. (See photograph on page 135.)

1   Trim the ends of the broccoli rabe and remove any large thick stems. Rinse well and shake off excess water.

2   Add the oil and garlic to a large straight-sided sauté pan; heat over medium heat. Add the red pepper flakes and broccoli rabe, salt generously, and cover immediately. Once the leaves wilt, less than 1 minute, turn them using tongs. Add the stock and increase the heat to medium-high. Sauté until the stock nearly evaporates, about 8 minutes. Transfer to a plate and drizzle with oil just before serving.

INDULGE

DESSERT IS THE GREAT UNIFIER. JUST ABOUT EVERYONE LOVES DESSERT.

I love making desserts, and always have. The very first recipe I ever tried was for Kris Kringle cookies from the *Weekly Reader*, when I was in the first grade. I couldn't wait to get home and try it. I spent my childhood baking, using my mother's Mixmaster from the fifties, which is still alive, if not all that well. A certain nostalgia for those early attempts of mine comes over me when I see that old mixer.

These days a workhorse of a Kitchenaid mixer sits on my counter, and while I use it often, I have a penchant for desserts that are simple. I like doing things by hand when possible, since it's often faster, and certainly more tactile. I enjoy the feeling of running my hands through a bowl of cool flour, and don't mind whipping a little cream by hand. When something needs very thorough mixing, such as a cheesecake batter, or vigorous whipping, such as a meringue, I turn to my mixer. If you don't have the room in the budget for a standing mixer, a handheld mixer can be used.

When it's time to choose a dessert to go with a menu, there are several factors to consider. Seasonality is one of them, and summer offers what seems like an endless variety of fruit, starting with strawberries in mid-June and ending with Italian prune plums in September. As summer fades into fall, apples, pears, and dried fruit are abundant. Pay attention to the market and the rhythm of the seasons in all your cooking, and that includes dessert. Nothing is more delicious and refreshing in August than an old-fashioned Peach Melba. Juicy peaches are simply peeled and cut up, and lay-

ered in a glass with a briefly cooked raspberry sauce and vanilla ice cream from the supermarket. It is heavenly, but it is a seasonal treat, since it highlights the natural beauty of fresh peaches.

The fruit dessert recipes work best with fruit that's in season. Peaches from halfway across the world in winter will not have the same flavor, texture, or juiciness as ones from your farmers' market in July. See what's in season before choosing a recipe, rather than the other way around. Even when using seasonal fruit, adjustments may need to be made to cooking times and amounts of thickeners. If the fruit for a crisp or tart seems exceptionally ripe and juicy, increase the amount of flour in the recipe by a tablespoon or two.

Think of dessert as part of the meal, not an afterthought. Dessert should complement the rest of the menu both in flavor and in theme. If I'm making a rustic Italian meal of Rigatoni with Squash and Caramelized Onions, I'll want a dessert like Roasted Pears to complement it. Boeuf Bourguignon, the French beef stew, calls for Caramel Apple Tart, my right-side-up variation on tarte Tatin. If the meal is a bit heavy or rich, then the dessert should be relatively light and refreshing.

These homey desserts are easy and not particularly time-consuming to prepare. Some are meant to be eaten that day, such as Grilled Stone Fruit or Chocolate Bread Pudding; others keep well for several days, such as Lemon Curd Cheesecake or Little Black Dress Cake. Enjoy them. What's life without a little indulgence?

ALMOND SHORTBREAD

MAKES ABOUT 3 DOZEN

½ cup (1¾ ounces) sliced almonds,
preferably unblanched, plus more for
garnish

¼ cup packed light brown sugar

1 stick (8 tablespoons) unsalted butter,
at room temperature

¼ cup granulated sugar, plus more for
garnish

½ teaspoon pure vanilla extract

½ teaspoon kosher or coarse or fine sea salt

1¼ cups all-purpose flour, measured,
then sifted

1 large egg white, lightly beaten with a fork

Such a simple cookie, but it never fails to satisfy. What makes shortbread unique is the play between sweet and salty. If you like coming across little pockets of saltiness, as I do, use coarse sea salt or kosher salt, otherwise use fine salt.

1 | Grind the nuts in a mini food processor or coffee grinder. Be careful not to overprocess them. Line a baking sheet with parchment paper or a reusable silicone baking mat. Pass the brown sugar through a sieve to remove any lumps.

2 | Cream together the butter, brown sugar, and granulated sugar until smooth. (I like to use a heavy bowl and a wooden spoon for this task.) Add the vanilla and salt and stir to combine. Mix in the nuts and finally the flour. Stir until the flour is completely incorporated; knead the dough a few times with your hands. The dough will be quite thick.

3 | Divide the dough into two equal pieces and set one half aside. Roll between 2 pieces of plastic wrap until about ¼ inch thick. (If you find the dough too soft to work with, flatten it into thick disks and wrap each piece in plastic wrap, then refrigerate for a short time until chilled, and try again. At this point the dough can also be frozen for a month or two.) Cut using a 2-inch cookie cutter and place about 1 inch apart on the prepared baking sheet. Excess dough can be rerolled. Repeat with the second half of the dough. Refrigerate until the cookies are well chilled.

4 | Preheat the oven to 300°F, and position the rack in the middle of the oven. Brush each cookie very sparingly with egg white. Press a few almond slices onto each cookie and sprinkle lightly with sugar. Bake until the cookies just begin to brown on the edges, 20 to 25 minutes, rotating the pan after about 10 minutes. Carefully transfer the shortbread to a wire cooling rack and cool completely. They will keep in an airtight container for several days.

> The weight of the nuts is important in this recipe. If you have a kitchen scale, use it. If you don't, and you are starting out with whole almonds instead of sliced, grind the almonds first, then measure out ½ cup (½ cup whole almonds = 2¼ ounces; ½ cup sliced almonds = 1¾ ounces; ½ cup ground almonds = 1¾ ounces).

CHOCOLATE-CHOCOLATE CHIP COOKIES

MAKES ABOUT 3 DOZEN

1 cup pecan halves, optional

2 cups plus 2 tablespoons all-purpose flour

½ teaspoon kosher salt

½ teaspoon baking soda

2 sticks (1 cup) unsalted butter

1 cup plus 2 tablespoons firmly packed dark
  brown sugar

½ cup granulated sugar

1 large egg plus 1 large egg yolk

½ tablespoon pure vanilla extract

1½ cups semisweet chocolate morsels

This is an adaptation of my friend Carolynn Carreño's fantastic chocolate chip cookies. These cookies are studded with chocolate and streaked with it, too.

1   If using pecans, preheat the oven to 375°F. Spread the nuts on a large baking sheet and place in the oven. Shake the pan every few minutes so the nuts toast evenly and do not burn, about 8 minutes total. Immediately transfer the nuts to a bowl and set aside.

2   In a large bowl, whisk together the flour, salt, and baking soda; set aside. Melt the butter in a medium saucepan over medium heat. Turn off the heat, add the sugars, and whisk until well combined.

3   Whisk the egg, egg yolk, and vanilla into the butter mixture slowly. Stir into the flour mixture until just combined. While the mixture is still warm, stir in the chocolate chips and nuts; let sit 30 seconds, then stir a few more times with a wooden spoon until the dough is streaked with chocolate but some whole chips remain. Divide the dough into two, flatten into disks or logs and wrap in plastic. Refrigerate until the dough is well chilled, several hours or overnight.

4   Preheat the oven to 325°F and position a rack in the middle of the oven. Line a baking sheet with parchment paper or a reusable silicone baking mat. Let the dough soften until malleable. Break or cut off dough into golf-ball-size chunks and, using your hands, shape into rough mounds. Place 3 inches apart on the baking sheet. Bake until the cookies are just set, 11 to 13 minutes. They will spread as they bake. Cool for 2 minutes on the cookie sheet, then transfer to a wire rack.

>   To make a batch of dough to keep on hand in the freezer, roll the dough into a 2-inch-diameter log to slice off as needed. Wrap tightly in plastic wrap, then thaw until soft enough to cut off 1-inch-thick slices. Let the slices of dough sit on a baking sheet until nearly thawed, and bake as directed above.

SAUCEPAN BROWNIES

MAKES 16 TO 25

1 stick (8 tablespoons) unsalted butter

4 ounces (4 squares) unsweetened
    chocolate, chopped

1¾ cup sugar

¼ teaspoon kosher or fine sea salt

1 teaspoon pure vanilla extract

2 large eggs

1 cup all-purpose flour

1 scant cup walnuts, broken into large
    pieces, optional

I tinkered endlessly with the proportions of basic brownie ingredients to come up with a recipe that I think is perfect. They have a deep chocolate flavor, moist, fudgy interior, and chewy edges. Best of all, they are entirely mixed in one saucepan. No bowls to wash!

1 | Preheat the oven to 350°F, and position a rack in the middle of the oven.

2 | Melt the butter in a medium saucepan over low heat. Turn off the heat, add the chocolate, and stir occasionally until melted and combined. Set aside and cool slightly.

3 | Stir the sugar and salt into the warm chocolate mixture, using a wooden spoon. Add the vanilla and eggs, one at a time, mixing well after each addition. Stir in the flour until just incorporated. Fold in the nuts, if using. Pour the mixture into an 8 × 8-inch nonstick baking pan, and smooth the surface using your hands. Bake 30 to 35 minutes, until the center is firm. Cool completely. When ready to serve, remove the brownies from the pan and cut into 1½- to 2-inch squares, or larger if you like.

> If you don't have a pan with a nonstick coating, line a pan with parchment paper or foil to make sure the brownies come out easily.

SERVES 6

½ large honeydew melon, peeled
    and seeded

1 seedless cucumber, peeled and cut
    into chunks

Juice of ½ lime

¼ cup superfine sugar, plus more to taste

Pour this slush into small glasses and pass on a tray between the main course and dessert.

1 | Cut the honeydew into 2-inch chunks and freeze until hard. Remove the melon from the freezer about 20 minutes before blending.

2 | Place the cucumber in a bar blender along with ¼ cup water, the lime juice, and ¼ cup sugar. Add the frozen honeydew chunks slowly, making sure they are well combined before adding more. Blend until completely smooth. Add additional sugar to taste, and serve immediately in chilled glasses.

BLUEBERRY CORNMEAL CROSTATAS

MAKES 8

Cornmeal Tart Dough (recipe follows)

2 pints blueberries, picked over

½ cup sugar

1 tablespoon all-purpose flour

Zest of 1 lemon, chopped

Juice of ½ lemon

The crunchiness of cornmeal dough is ideal for rustic fruit tarts. This free-form wrapper for fresh blueberries makes a tart that's Italian in spirit.

1 | Remove the dough from the refrigerator about 30 minutes before rolling.

2 | Combine the blueberries, sugar, flour, lemon zest, and lemon juice in a large bowl. Toss together gently and set aside.

3 | When the dough is malleable but still firm, cut each disk into quarters. Working quickly, use your hands to form a ball with one piece of dough. Flatten the ball and place between 2 pieces of plastic wrap. Roll out into a circle 5 to 6 inches in diameter and about ⅛-inch thick. Leave it in the plastic wrap and place the rolled dough on a plate. Transfer to the refrigerator. Continue to roll out the remaining dough putting each in the refrigerator as you finish. Chill until firm but still workable.

4 | Line a large baking sheet with parchment paper. Place a circle of dough on the baking sheet, leaving room for the other crostatas. Spoon about ½ cup of the berry mixture onto the circle, leaving at least a 1-inch border. Bring the edges of the dough over the top to envelop the berries. Using your hands, fold in the edges, pressing gently and patching any holes. Cup your hands over the tart and press down firmly to shape. Repeat with remaining dough and berries. Chill for about 20 minutes before baking. While the tarts are chilling, preheat the oven to 375°F.

5 | Bake until the crust turns golden brown and the fruit is bubbling, about 25 minutes. Let set for 5 to 10 minutes before transferring from baking sheet to serving plates. Serve warm or at room temperature with vanilla ice cream or Homemade Crème Fraîche (page 29).

1⅓ cups all-purpose flour

½ cup cornmeal

½ teaspoon kosher or fine
  sea salt

1¼ sticks (10 tablespoons)
  unsalted butter, at room
  temperature

½ cup sugar

3 large egg yolks

½ teaspoon pure vanilla
  extract

CORNMEAL TART DOUGH

This tart dough is almost like cookie dough. It can't be worked when it is ice cold, but it shouldn't be too warm, either. It's a bit fragile, but thankfully very easy to patch.

1 Combine the flour, cornmeal, and salt in a bowl. Whisk to combine and set aside.

2 Cream together the butter and sugar. Stir in the yolks, one at a time, making sure each one is well combined before adding the next. Add the vanilla and mix well. Sift the dry ingredients over the wet ingredients and stir to combine until the dough forms a ball.

3 Divide the dough in two and pat into flat disks. Wrap each disk tightly in plastic wrap and chill or freeze until ready to use.

CARAMEL APPLE TART

SERVES 6 TO 8

1 cup sugar

3 tablespoons unsalted butter,
    cut into pieces

4 Granny Smith apples, peeled, cored,
    and each cut into 8 wedges

½ vanilla bean, or 1 teaspoon pure vanilla
    extract

Flour, for rolling

½ recipe Flaky Tart Dough (page 33)

1 large egg yolk

1 tablespoon heavy cream or milk

Homemade Crème Fraîche (page 29)

Too often the apples become soggy in a tarte Tatin, the famous upside-down apple tart. By turning the tart right side up again, the apples retain their firmness with an almost candied consistency. It's the ultimate combination of flaky pastry and pure apple flavor.

1   Make the caramelized apples: Stir together ⅔ cup water and the sugar in a large, heavy, light-colored frying or sauté pan no smaller than 10 inches. After this point, do not stir: just swirl the pan gently to keep the caramel cooking evenly. If you notice undissolved sugar on the sides of the pan, brush them down with water to prevent crystallization.

2   Cook over medium-high heat, swirling occasionally. As the caramel begins to darken, swirl more frequently to even out the color. Cook until the sugar is a dark amber color, 15 to 20 minutes, depending on the size and weight of the pan. If the sugar is cooking too quickly, reduce the heat to medium.

3   As soon as the caramel is ready, add the butter, immediately followed by the apples. The caramel will sputter a bit when the apples are added, so do so carefully. Toss well to combine.

4   Scrape the seeds from the vanilla bean half into the apple mixture and add the pod. Stir well to combine. Continue cooking over medium-high heat until the apples begin to turn transparent around the edges, about 15 minutes. After the initial stir, it is important that you gently toss the apples, rather than stir, so the apples do not fall apart. When the apples are done, turn off the heat. Add the vanilla extract, if using, and toss a few times. Immediately transfer the apples to a nonstick baking sheet. Using a wooden spoon, gently spread them into a single layer and let cool.

5   Line a baking sheet with parchment paper. On a lightly floured surface, roll the dough, working from the center out, into roughly a 14- × 16-inch rectangle. The dough should be no more than ¼ inch thick. Every few rolls, release the dough by running an offset spatula underneath, and sprinkle more flour under it. Drape the dough over a rolling pin and transfer to the baking sheet.

6 | Arrange the apples in the center of the dough leaving a 1½-inch border. (If the caramel has hardened you can loosen it by placing the baking sheet in the oven for a few minutes.) Gently fold the edge of the crust up and over the apples, tearing off any excess dough if it's covering too much of the filling. There should be approximately a 2-inch edge of dough on all sides, with the center open. Refrigerate or freeze until firm.

7 | While the tart is chilling, preheat the oven to 375°F and position a rack in the middle of the oven.

8 | Whisk together the egg yolk and cream, and brush lightly on the edge of the tart. Bake the tart, rotating the pan halfway through, until the crust is golden and the apples are bubbling, about 35 minutes. Transfer to a wire rack and cool slightly. Serve warm or at room temperature with Homemade Crème Fraîche (page 29).

MAKING CARAMEL

Making caramel is actually very easy, but you might mess it up once or twice before you get it right. Don't be afraid to experiment—it's only sugar.

- Caramel is very hot. Wear an oven mitt when tossing or stirring and don't touch the caramel while it's cooking.

- Choose a pan that's light colored inside (preferably stainless steel) so you can see the caramel change color.

- If you don't have a light-colored pan, you can do a quick test by sticking a light colored spoon in the caramel as it cooks, or by placing a few drops on a piece of white paper.

- It is critical that you have the butter, vanilla, and apples prepared and ready to use before you start cooking the caramel. Adding the cold butter will slow the cooking process.

- Caramel can go from just right to burned rather quickly, so err a little on the undercooked side if you're unsure when to stop. It will get a little darker once the apples have been added.

SERVES 10 TO 12

FOR THE GRAHAM CRACKER CRUST

1¼ cups graham cracker crumbs

    (about 9 crackers)

3 tablespoons sugar

⅛ teaspoon kosher or fine sea salt

5 tablespoons unsalted butter, melted

FOR THE FILLING

2½ packages (8 ounces each)

    regular cream cheese

½ cup plus 2 tablespoons sugar

3 tablespoons all-purpose flour

Pinch of kosher salt

1 teaspoon pure vanilla extract

1 teaspoon freshly squeezed lemon juice

1 teaspoon freshly grated lemon zest

2 large eggs plus 1 large egg yolk

½ cup sour cream

Melted unsalted butter for the pan

Lemon Curd (recipe follows)

I am tempted to call this cheesecake a tart, because it has about half the amount of cream cheese filling as a regular cheesecake. The thick layer of lemon curd is a tart counterpoint to the creamy filling, creating a Creamsicle-like effect. Adults and children are equally enthusiastic about this cake.

1   Preheat the oven to 350°F, and position a rack in the middle of the oven. Prepare a 9-inch springform pan by cutting a parchment circle to fit the bottom of the pan.

2   Make the crust: Combine the graham cracker crumbs, sugar, and salt in a small bowl. Stir in the melted butter with a fork until well combined. Press the mixture evenly into the bottom of the prepared pan. Bake for 10 minutes. Cool on a wire rack while you prepare the filling.

3   Lower the oven temperature to 325°F. Beat the cream cheese at medium-low speed in an electric standing mixer fitted with the paddle attachment about 2 minutes, until creamy. With the mixer on low, gradually add the sugar, then the flour, and finally a pinch of salt. With a spatula scrape down the sides of the bowl and paddle twice.

4   Switch to the whisk attachment and continue, mixing in the vanilla, lemon juice, and lemon zest. Whip in the eggs, one at a time, and then add the yolk, scraping the bowl and whisking at least twice. Continue to whip on low speed and add the sour cream. Whip until well blended. Do not overbeat. The batter should be light and airy.

5   Brush the sides of the springform pan with melted butter. Wrap the pan tightly in heavy-duty aluminum foil, making sure there are no holes in the foil. Pour the filling into the pan. Place the springform in a large roasting pan and pour hot tap water into the roasting pan so that it comes about halfway up the springform. Transfer carefully to the oven and bake until the filling is just set, about 45 minutes. If the edges start to pull away from the sides of the pan sooner than that, remove it from the oven. Immediately remove the pan from the water and remove the foil. Place on a wire rack and cool to room temperature.

6 Warm the lemon curd until it is pourable and spread it over the surface of the cheesecake. Tilt from side to side to form an even layer. Cover the springform with plastic wrap and refrigerate for 8 hours or overnight. To unmold the cake, place a hot towel around the pan to loosen the cake from the pan. Run a butter knife around the edges and remove the outer part of the pan. To serve, slide the cake onto a serving plate with the parchment.

> It is essential to have all of the filling ingredients, especially the cream cheese, at room temperature. To speed the softening, cut the cream cheese into pieces and let sit in the bowl while you prepare the crust.

> To slice the cheesecake neatly, run a large knife under very hot water, and dry with a cloth. Make a cut, and repeat for each slice.

MAKES ABOUT 2 CUPS

½ cup freshly squeezed
    lemon juice

6 large egg yolks

1 cup sugar

4 teaspoons freshly grated
    lemon zest

1 stick (8 tablespoons) cold
    unsalted butter, cut into
    1-inch pieces

LEMON CURD

Lemon curd goes back and forth between a liquid and solid state depending on its temperature, since it has quite a bit of butter in it. If you're using it to smoothly glaze the top of a cake, or to pour into a prebaked tart shell, lemon curd should be warm. It will spread out all on its own to a smooth-as-glass surface. Chilled, it will be firm enough to slice.

1 Combine the lemon juice, egg yolks, and sugar in a nonreactive bowl. Whisk until smooth. Transfer the mixture to a heavy nonreactive saucepan and cook over medium heat, stirring constantly with a wooden spoon, until hot, 5 to 10 minutes. The mixture should begin to thicken as the temperature increases. Once thick (it should coat the back of the spoon), reduce the heat and cook for an additional 5 to 10 minutes, stirring continuously.

2 Remove the saucepan from the heat and strain the curd into a bowl. Stir in the lemon zest and butter until the butter has completely melted. Cool slightly before using. The curd can be stored in the refrigerator in an airtight container up to 1 week. Warm over a double boiler or microwave briefly to return it to liquid form. It will set up again when chilled.

PAVLOVAS WITH STRAWBERRIES AND CREAM

SERVES 8

FOR THE MERINGUES

2 tablespoons cornstarch

1¼ cups superfine sugar

6 large egg whites

Pinch of fine sea salt

Dash of pure vanilla extract

1½ teaspoons white vinegar

FOR SERVING

1 quart strawberries (2 pints), cleaned, hulled, and halved if large

¼ cup sugar

1 tablespoon kirsch (cherry brandy) or Cognac

½ pint heavy (whipping) cream

Dash of pure vanilla extract

This ethereal dessert, with its combination of crisp-chewy meringue, soft, light whipped cream, and sweet, fragrant strawberries, is pure heaven. The meringues in this version are chewy and marshmallow-like. Make them on a dry June day when local strawberries are in season.

1 | Preheat the oven to 300°F and position a rack in the middle of the oven. Line 2 baking sheets with parchment paper or reusable silicone baking mats.

2 | Make the meringues: Combine the cornstarch and ¼ cup sugar in a bowl and set aside. Beat the egg whites and salt in an electric standing mixer fitted with the whisk attachment on low speed, increasing it to high as the eggs start to foam. Once the eggs begin to come together add the remaining 1 cup sugar, 1 tablespoon at a time. Beat the eggs on high until stiff, shiny peaks form.

3 | Remove the bowl from the mixer and fold in the vanilla and the vinegar. Sift the sugar-cornstarch mixture over the egg whites a little at a time, folding gently after each addition. Spoon the meringue in ½-cup dollops onto the baking sheets, leaving ample space between each of them. Using a soupspoon, create a depression on the tops. Bake for 10 minutes, then lower the temperature to 225°F. Bake for 1 hour. Turn off the oven and cool in the oven for several hours or overnight. They should be on two racks of the oven, evenly spaced.

4 | Toss the strawberries with the sugar and kirsch and macerate (let sit) at room temperature until the berries begin to exude their juices. This can take anywhere from 30 minutes to 2 hours, depending on the ripeness of the berries.

5 | Just before serving, whip the cream using a chilled metal bowl and whisk. When it begins to thicken, add the vanilla. Continue to whip until soft peaks form.

6 Place one meringue on each dessert plate. Top each one with a dollop of whipped cream and a spoonful of berries. Serve immediately.

> It's crucial that your bowl and whip are completely grease-free so your meringues can reach their maximum volume. The tiniest bit of grease—whether from a bit of egg yolk or a buttery bowl—will keep the egg whites from whipping into a foam. I clean my bowl and whip with a bit of white vinegar or lemon juice to make sure they're clean.

> Cold eggs separate more easily, but warm ones whip better, so separate the eggs when they're cold. Use your clean hands to gently hold the yolk, and let the whites drip through your fingers into a clean bowl. Then cover the bowl of whites with plastic wrap and let it warm up a bit before whipping them. The yolks can be saved for another use, such as Lemon Curd (page 231).

GRILLED STONE FRUIT

SERVES 6

2 tablespoons unsalted butter, melted

2 tablespoons light brown sugar

Dash of pure vanilla extract

3 peaches, cut in half, with pits removed

3 plums, cut in half, with pits removed

¼ pound cherries, stems intact

When peaches, nectarines, apricots, plums, and cherries are cooked on the grill, they become juicy and caramelized. A layer of heavy-duty aluminum foil separates the fruit from the direct heat of the grill—and the grates you just cooked your fish, or steaks, or chicken on. Serve warm with vanilla ice cream or mascarpone cheese.

1 In a medium bowl, combine the butter, sugar, and vanilla. Toss the fruit in the butter mixture and let macerate for 15 minutes. Make a large tray from heavy-duty foil: Fold a large piece in half and turn up the edges to form a ½-inch edge all around.

2 Heat a charcoal, gas, or indoor grill to medium-hot. Arrange the fruit, cut side down, on the foil tray. When the fruit turns golden brown and juices begin to exude, turn over. This will take 5 to 10 minutes depending on the temperature of the grill. Grill on the reverse side for an additional 2 to 3 minutes. Remove the pieces to a platter as they are done.

SERVES 8

1 loaf brioche or challah (12 to 16 ounces),
     or 6 to 8 individual brioches, about
     2 ounces each

2 cups milk

1 cup heavy cream

8 ounces bittersweet chocolate,
     broken into small pieces

6 large egg yolks

½ cup granulated sugar

1 teaspoon pure vanilla extract

2 tablespoons unsweetened cocoa powder

Pinch of kosher or fine sea salt

1 tablespoon Cognac or brandy

Confectioners' sugar for sprinkling

Use light, airy bread such as brioche loaf, individual brioches, or challah for this recipe or the custard won't be absorbed properly. Buy about one pound total, so that once trimmed, you have about twelve ounces for the pudding.

1   Trim the crusts from the large loaves, or just the bottom crust from the individual brioches. If using loaves, slice into ½-inch slices. If using individual brioches, cut them crosswise into ½-inch-thick circles. The slices from the bottom of the individual brioches will be flower-shaped. Separate those from the rest and set aside.

2   Combine the milk and cream in a small saucepan and scald (heat until just below boiling) over medium-high heat. Add the chocolate and let sit for 5 minutes. Stir until completely combined. Set aside.

3   Whisk the yolks, granulated sugar, and vanilla in a large bowl until pale yellow. Whisk in the cocoa. Add the salt and Cognac and stir to combine. Gradually whisk the warm chocolate mixture into the egg mixture. Do not add the chocolate mixture too quickly or the eggs will cook.

4   Dip 4 to 5 slices of bread in the chocolate custard at a time, turning them as if you were making French toast, and letting each piece sit for about 1 minute in the custard. Once soaked, transfer to a 2-quart ceramic or ovenproof porcelain baking dish. (If using individual brioches, dip the "flower" brioche slices last so they form a decorative top.) Continue until all the slices have been dipped and layered in the baking dish. Pour any remaining custard over the top, cover with aluminum foil, and let sit for 30 minutes. Preheat the oven to 325°F and position a rack in the middle of the oven.

5   Place the baking dish in a larger roasting pan and fill with enough hot tap water to reach halfway up the sides. Bake for 45 minutes, or until the center is just beginning to set. Remove the aluminum foil and bake

for an additional 10 minutes. Carefully remove from the oven and let cool for 10 minutes in the water bath. Dust with confectioners' sugar and serve warm.

> The exact size of the baking dish is not absolutely crucial in this recipe, as long as the bread and custard fill the dish nearly to the top. You can even divide it among individual ramekins or custard cups, which takes no more work than one big dish. You will have to adjust the baking time accordingly. It will bake faster in individual ramekins or a larger-diameter dish, since the pudding will be shallower. A smaller-diameter, deeper dish may take longer. Either way, the center should be just set when done.

STRAWBERRY-RHUBARB CRISP

SERVES 6 TO 8

1 quart (2 pints) strawberries, washed,
　　hulled, and halved if large

1 pound rhubarb stalks, cut into
　　¾-inch pieces

½ cup sugar

2 tablespoons all-purpose flour

Zest of 1 orange, grated, optional

Crisp Topping (page 242)

I am always amazed at how easy it is to make people happy with a fruit crisp for dessert. Who can resist warm, fragrant fruit with a sweet and crunchy topping? It's my favorite way to celebrate the fruit of the moment. A scoop of vanilla ice cream or a dollop of Homemade Crème Fraîche (page 29) makes it even better.

Preheat the oven to 375°F. In a large bowl, combine the strawberries, rhubarb, sugar, flour, and orange zest, if using. Toss gently to combine. Transfer to a shallow 2-quart baking dish or individual ramekins. Spread the topping generously over the fruit and place on a baking sheet. Bake for about 35 to 45 minutes, or 25 to 30 minutes for individual crisps, until the topping is brown and the juices are bubbling. Serve warm.

SERVES 6 TO 8

1½ cups dry red wine

¼ cup honey

¼ cup sugar

1 cinnamon stick

½ teaspoon finely ground black pepper

1 bay leaf

½ vanilla bean, scraped

1 cup dried figs

4 Anjou or Bartlett pears, ripe but firm

4 Granny Smith apples

½ cup dried cherries or cranberries

1 tablespoon all-purpose flour

Crisp Topping (recipe follows)

There is a little more work involved here than with your average fruit crisp, but the results are well worth it. The filling takes on a sophisticated air with the addition of red wine, which turns into a heady sauce for the fruit. Serve warm with Homemade Crème Fraîche (page 29) or vanilla ice cream.

1   Bring the wine, honey, sugar, cinnamon, pepper, bay leaf, and vanilla bean pod and seeds to a boil in a medium saucepan. Stir well. Reduce heat to low, and simmer, uncovered, for about 10 minutes, skimming any foam that rises to the top. Cut the figs in half lengthwise if they are small or in quarters if large and set aside. Add the figs to the poaching liquid.

2   Peel the pears. Cut into quarters and remove the cores and stems. Cut each quarter into 3 or 4 chunks.

3   Add the pears to the poaching liquid and cook very gently at a bare simmer over medium heat until the pears are tender, stirring occasionally, 5 to 10 minutes, depending on the ripeness of the pears.

4   Preheat the oven to 375°F. Pour the poached fruit into a strainer over a bowl. Transfer the pears and figs to a large bowl. Discard the cinnamon, bay leaf, and vanilla bean. Return the poaching liquid to the saucepan and reduce the liquid over medium-high heat until it turns thick and syrupy, 10 to 15 minutes (reduce to ½ cup). Peel the apples and cut into quarters. Remove the cores then cut each quarter into 5 slices and set aside.

5 Add the apples, cherries, flour, and reduced poaching liquid to the pears and figs. Gently toss so that the mixture is well combined. Transfer to a shallow 3-quart baking dish and sprinkle the crisp topping evenly over the top. Bake for 35 to 45 minutes, until the topping is brown and the juices are bubbling. Transfer to a wire rack to cool slightly.

CRISP TOPPING

This topping is exceptionally crunchy. Add a touch of nutmeg or cardamom if you like. If the fruit you are using seems extra juicy, add more flour to the fruit so the topping doesn't sink into it.

Combine the flour, brown sugar, granulated sugar, cinnamon, and salt in a medium bowl. Stir with a whisk or fork until well combined; then rub between your thumbs to eliminate lumps. Rub the butter pieces into the dry ingredients by rolling them between your thumb and fingers until the butter is thoroughly incorporated, and small- to medium-size crumbs form. Add the oats or nuts, if using. Work in briefly using your fingers. Chill until firm, at least 30 minutes. The topping can be frozen for several weeks or refrigerated for a few days at this point, stored in an airtight container or a resealable plastic bag.

MAKES ABOUT 3 CUPS

1 cup plus 2 tablespoons
    all-purpose flour

⅓ cup packed dark or light
    brown sugar

½ cup granulated sugar

¾ teaspoon ground
    cinnamon

¼ teaspoon kosher salt

1 stick (8 tablespoons) cold
    unsalted butter, cut into
    small pieces

½ cup quick-cooking oats or
    chopped nuts, optional

CREMA CATALANA

SERVES 4

2 cups milk

Two 1-inch strips lemon peel, pith removed

1 cinnamon stick

A few gratings of fresh nutmeg

4 large egg yolks

About 7 tablespoons sugar

2 tablespoons cornstarch

The creme brûlée of Spain is a bit lighter since it is made with milk, not cream. Also, it is infused with cinnamon, nutmeg, and lemon, rather than vanilla. Using a salamander, which is like a branding iron, to make the crackly layer of burnt sugar is traditional, but they are hard to find here. I bought one for about two dollars in a hardware store in Barcelona, and love using it, but a kitchen blowtorch can be used, too.

1 Bring the milk to a boil with the lemon peel, cinnamon, and nutmeg in a small saucepan. Remove from the heat, cover, and steep 10 minutes. Discard the lemon peel and cinnamon. Whisk the egg yolks and 3 tablespoons of the sugar until pale yellow. Add the cornstarch and whisk until combined.

2 Temper the eggs by adding a few tablespoons of the hot milk and mixing well. Then add the egg mixture back to the rest of the milk. Cook over medium heat, whisking constantly, for about 5 minutes, until the mixture thickens and is smooth. (Don't let it come to a boil.) Pour the custard into a bowl and whisk vigorously to release the steam.

3 Pour the custard into four 4-ounce ramekins. Let cool to room temperature, then cover with plastic wrap and refrigerate 2 hours or overnight.

4 Evenly sprinkle about 1 tablespoon of sugar (more if your ramekins are wide, less if they are narrow) over the top of each of the custards. Caramelize the sugar by slowly and steadily going back and forth over the sugar with a mini blowtorch until the sugar begins to bubble and then brown. Be careful not to get the flame too close or the sugar will burn. Serve immediately.

> Use a small sieve to sprinkle the sugar over the custard. It will caramelize more evenly.

PEACH MELBA

SERVES 6

1 pint raspberries

½ cup sugar

6 ripe peaches

About 1 pint vanilla ice cream

Almond Shortbread (page 214)

A sublime and classic dessert that belies its simplicity. Serve in pretty stemmed glasses or tumblers for a refined presentation accompanied by Almond Shortbread. This dessert should be reserved for juicy, ripe in-season peaches, but if for some reason they aren't as flavorful as you'd like, sprinkle the peaches with a little sugar and a few drops of liqueur such as kirsch, Cognac, or use a white dessert wine such as muscat de Beaumes-de-Venise, which would also go very nicely with it.

1   Combine half of the raspberries, the sugar, and 1 tablespoon water in a small saucepan. Stir over medium heat until the sugar melts and the mixture comes to a boil, about 5 minutes. Turn off the heat and fold in the remaining raspberries and transfer to a bowl to cool. (This can be made several days in advance and stored in an airtight container in the refrigerator.)

2   Cut a shallow X into the bottom of each peach with a paring knife. Plunge the peaches into boiling water for about 30 seconds (or until the skins loosen), and then into ice water. Slip off the skins and cut each peach into 6 to 8 slices.

3   To serve, place 1 sliced peach in each of 6 stemmed glasses or tumblers. Place about ¼ cup raspberry sauce on top, and top with one generous scoop of ice cream. Serve immediately with Almond Shortbread.

ROASTED PEARS WITH RED WINE

SERVES 6

6 Bosc, Bartlett, or Anjou pears,
    stems intact

½ cup golden raisins

½ cup currants

About 3 teaspoons unsalted butter,
    at room temperature

½ cup sugar

1½ cups dry red wine, preferably
    a good Italian Chianti

1 bay leaf

2 or 3 cinnamon sticks

Finely ground black pepper

Ricotta

This is a not-too-sweet and not-too-sinful dessert that goes especially well with Italian menus in fall and winter. The roasting time will vary depending on the ripeness of the pears.

1   Preheat the oven to 400°F. Trim the bottoms of the pears slightly so that they will stand upright and peel the top halves with a paring knife or vegetable peeler. Core the pears from the bottom using a melon baller. Stuff the bottoms with the raisins and currants (you won't need all of them).

2   Arrange the pears in a 9- × 13-inch baking pan. Rub the top of each pear with ½ teaspoon of butter. Sprinkle the sugar evenly over the pears. Pour the wine into the pan. Add the bay leaf, cinnamon sticks, a large pinch of pepper, and the remaining raisins and currants and place in the oven.

3   Roast 30 minutes to 1 hour, basting every 10 to 15 minutes, until tender when pierced with the tip of a paring knife. The liquid will become quite syrupy. If the pears are tender before the syrup has reduced, carefully transfer the pears to a large plate and reduce the liquid in a saucepan over medium heat until it thickens. Once thick, return the pears and syrup to the baking pan. As they cool, continue to baste the pears frequently for 15 to 20 minutes. Transfer the pears to a platter and pour the syrup and raisins over them. Serve warm with the ricotta in a bowl on the side.

>   **Pears that are just beginning to ripen are perfect for this recipe. When shopping for them, test their ripeness by applying a little pressure right next to the stem. If it gives a little, they are perfect. If it doesn't give at all, they will be too hard.**

LITTLE BLACK DRESS CAKE

SERVES 10 TO 12

2 sticks (1 cup) unsalted butter, at room
temperature, plus more for pan

12 ounces bittersweet chocolate

1¼ cups granulated sugar

6 large eggs, separated

1 teaspoon pure vanilla extract

⅓ cup (1½ ounces) ground almonds or
hazelnuts (see below)

Pinch of kosher or fine sea salt

½ cup all-purpose flour

Confectioners' sugar, optional

Sour Cream Ganache (recipe follows),
optional

Just like that little black dress on hand for special occasions, everyone needs a stylish, simple, and goes-with-everything chocolate cake recipe like this one. Exceptionally moist with a rich chocolate flavor, this cake can be served while still a bit warm, with a simple dusting of confectioners' sugar. Or it can be cooled and inverted and spread with a contrastingly tart Sour Cream Ganache. It keeps very well for a couple of days at room temperature under a glass cake dome.

1   Preheat the oven to 350°F and position a rack in the middle of the oven. Prepare a 9-inch springform pan by brushing the bottom and sides with melted butter and cutting a parchment circle to fit the bottom of the pan. Brush the paper lightly with butter.

2   Place the chocolate in a small metal bowl. Bring a small saucepan of water to a boil, turn off the heat, and place the bowl on top. Stir occasionally until the chocolate is smooth. Set aside and cool slightly.

3   In a large mixing bowl, cream the butter with 1 cup sugar using a wooden spoon. Add the egg yolks, one at a time, stirring thoroughly after each addition. Add the vanilla and nuts and stir to combine.

4   Gradually stir the chocolate into the egg mixture. Combine thoroughly and set aside.

5   Beat the egg whites and salt in an electric standing mixer fitted with the whisk attachment on low speed, increasing it to high as the eggs start to foam. Slowly add the remaining ¼ cup sugar and continue to beat until soft peaks form. You can also do this with a handheld mixer in a medium bowl.

6   Whisk about one quarter of the egg whites into the chocolate mixture to lighten it. Add the remaining egg whites and sift the flour over the top. Using a large, preferably curved, rubber spatula, fold the ingredients until well combined. To fold, gently lift and scoop the mixture up from the bottom of the bowl over the top of the ingredients. At the same time rotate the bowl a quarter turn each time you fold. Continue until there are almost no white or chocolate streaks in the batter. Pour the batter into the prepared pan, smooth the surface, and bake for 30 to

35 minutes, until it cracks slightly and rises into a slight dome. Transfer to a wire rack to cool. Cool completely if icing. It will fall a bit as it cools.

7 To unmold the cake, run a butter knife around the edges and remove the outer part of the pan. To serve as is, slide onto a serving plate and dust the top with confectioners' sugar. If icing, invert onto a flat serving plate, and peel off the parchment. Pour all of the ganache onto the top of the cake. Using a small offset or rubber spatula, spread the ganache in soft swirls over the top and sides of the cake.

> To grind the nuts, toast them first (according to directions on page 32) and cool completely. Pulse in a coffee grinder or mini food processor until finely ground. Be careful not to overprocess into a butter.

If you don't have a kitchen scale, buy two three- to four-ounce chocolate bars, rather than large chunks, so you can easily estimate the weight by eye.

MAKES ENOUGH FOR

A 9-INCH CAKE

6 ounces bittersweet
    chocolate

8 ounces sour cream

2 tablespoons unsalted
    butter, at room
    temperature

2 tablespoons light
    corn syrup

1 Place the chocolate in a small metal bowl. Bring a small saucepan of water to a boil, turn off the heat, and place the bowl on top. Stir occasionally until the chocolate is smooth. Set aside and cool slightly. Warm the sour cream, still in its container with the lid removed, in the microwave or in a bowl of warm water until just warm. Stir occasionally, changing the water as it cools. If the sour cream is cold, it will not blend smoothly with the chocolate. If it is hot, it may curdle, so you want it to be just warm.

2 Stir the sour cream into the chocolate. Add the butter, then the corn syrup. Stir until well combined. The ganache should be silky smooth. Let cool, stirring occasionally, until spreadable.

> Ganache, although it's made with heavy cream, or in this case sour cream, does not need refrigeration. The high sugar and fat content of the mixture prevents spoilage.

SOURCES

FOR UNUSUAL INGREDIENTS

D'Artagnan

280 Wilson Avenue

Newark, NJ 07105

800-327-8246 ext. 0

www.dartagnan.com

For poussins, demi-glace, mushrooms,

and much more

Kalustyan's

123 Lexington Avenue

New York, NY 10016

212-685-3451

www.kalustyans.com

For a wide variety of international ingredi-

ents including pumpkin seed oil, the

freshest nuts, dried fruit, vanilla beans,

Thai sauces, all kinds of spices and grains,

including Israeli couscous

La Tienda

3601 LaGrange Parkway

Toano, VA 23168

888-472-1022

www.tienda.com

For Spanish ingredients including smoked

paprika and paella supplies

Murray's Cheese Shop

257 Bleecker Street

New York, NY 10014

888-MY-CHEEZ

www.murrayscheese.com

For Parmigiano-Reggiano, buffalo moz-

zarella, ricotta salata, Taleggio, and

fontina cheeses.

Oliviers & Co.

www.oliviersandco.com

For olive oils and ready-made bouquets

garnis

Zingerman's Delicatessen

620 Phoenix Drive

Ann Arbor, MI 48108

888-636-8162

www.zingerman's.com

For cheese, oils, vinegars, smoked paprika,

and a wide variety of specialty ingredients

FOR SERVING DISHES,
DISHWARE, PLATTERS, AND
OTHER TABLETOP ACCESSORIES

Aero LTD

419 Broome Street

New York, NY 10013

212-966-1500

Armani Casa

97 Greene Street

New York, NY 10012

212-334-1271

www.armanicasa.com

Bloom

Sage & Madison Street

Sag Harbor, NY 11963

631-725-5940

Clio

92 Thompson Street

New York, NY 10012

212-966-8991

www.clio-home.com

Crate and Barrel

www.crateandbarrel.com

Dandelion

55 Potrero Avenue

San Francisco, CA 94103

415-436-9500

The Gardener

1836 Fourth Street

Berkeley, CA 94710

510-548-4545

www.thegardener.com

Global Table

107-109 Sullivan Street

New York, NY 10012

212-431-5839

www.globaltable.com

H. Groome

9 Main Street

Southampton, NY 11968

631-204-0491

Joan Platt Pottery

By appointment only

1261 Madison Avenue

New York, NY 10128

212-876-9228

Laurin Copen Antiques

1703 Montauk Highway

PO Box 34

Bridgehampton, NY 11932

631-537-2802

Lucca & Co
67 Gansevoort Street
New York, NY 10014
212-741-0400

ok
8303 West Third Street
Los Angeles, CA 90048
323-653-3501

Smith & Hawken
www.smithandhawken.com
For copper firepit

Sur La Table
www.surlatable.com

Sylvester & Co.
103 Main Street
Sag Harbor, NY 11963
631-725-5012

Takashimaya
693 Fifth Avenue
New York, NY 10022
212-350-0100

Williams-Sonoma
www.williams-sonoma.com

FOR KITCHEN TOOLS AND
EQUIPMENT

Bridge Kitchenware
711 Third Avenue (at 45th St.)

New York, NY 10022
1 800-274-3435 ext. 13
www.bridgekitchenware.com
For copper cookware and a wide variety of
tools, tart pans, gratin dishes, kitchen
blowtorches, ramekins, etc.

Crate and Barrel
www.crateandbarrel.com

Sur La Table
www.surlatable.com

Williams-Sonoma
www.williams-sonoma.com

There are many people I would like to give thanks to for helping me to turn this book into a reality. Without Janis Donnaud, my tenacious and supportive agent, this book would not be. She believed in me from the start and has guided me safely through uncharted territory with her wisdom and experience. To Harriet Bell, my patient and thorough editor, for her creative vision and confidence in me. Thank you, Harriet, for letting me do my thing. Also to Leah Carlson-Stanisic and everyone else at William Morrow for your support and enthusiasm for this project.

A huge heartfelt thanks to Maria Robledo, for your soulful photographs. You bring out the best in me, and made the entire experience of photographing the book a delightful one. To Kristine Foley for your steadfast assistance to Maria. It was great having you along. To David and Joleen Hughes at Level Design for taking on this book and anointing it with your top-notch design skills. Thanks Holton, for your spoons.

To Page Marchese Norman, prop stylist extraordinaire, for your incredible sense of style and beauty. You brought something so special to the book. Thank you for lending your impressive personal collection of props, including your own delicate ceramics. Thank you for flying across the country three times to be at the shoots. Thanks Ayesha and Jodi for that extra touch. For their assistance with props, thanks to Kristine Trevino, Sara Hotchkiss, and Simone Uranovsky. Also, thanks to Talia Kasher for helping me to see the obvious and for your astute observations.

To Jill Anton, my assistant, who helped me with every aspect of the book, from codifying recipes, testing them, keeping the manuscript organized, and organizing the shoots, to (of course) lots and lots of shopping. Thank you, Jill, for your dedication to this project—I couldn't have done it without you. To Barry, for your honest feedback on recipes. Thanks to Ann Robertson for helping out on the second shoot.

To my parents, who turned their home into a B&B on three separate occasions to help accommodate the crew, for all of your love and support throughout the years. Thanks to Frances Boswell and Andrew Pollock who also helped with accommodations, and to David and Aliana Spungen.

For your help with the cover shoot, many thanks to Amy and Adam Forbes, Suzanne Shaker, Kendra Livingstone, Kirsten Kjaer-Weis, and Mary Dail.

To the many stores and companies who lent us props, thank you. Special thanks to Carl and Steve at Tampopo in San Francisco; Bloom in Sag Harbor, NY; H. Groome in Southampton, NY; Laurin Copen Antiques and Gray Gardens Antiques in Bridgehampton, NY; Nathalie at Global Table; Ted and Lance at Lucca & Co; and Takashimaya, Aero, and Armani Casa in New York City. Thanks also to Meredith Bradford at Williams-Sonoma and to Joan Platt for your beautiful ceramics.

Thank you to Carolynn Carreño, Kathleen Hackett, and Celia Barbour for important bits of advice at crucial moments.

A very big thank-you goes to Martha Stewart for giving me the incredible opportunities and experiences that have gotten me where I am today. Thanks for giving me the confidence to do things differently, and for instilling in me the importance of logic and simplicity.

Last, and most important, thank you to Steven Kasher for being my best friend and biggest supporter. Thanks for putting up with my bouts of anxiety and keeping me on the straight and narrow. Also, thanks for your enthusiastic love of food, for being an expert grillmeister on the shoots, and for your all around good cheer.

INDEX

nuts:
    basic toasted, 32
    in little black dress cake, 251–52
    in roasted pear salad with Gorgonzola, 124
    see also specific nuts

oils, cooking, 126
olives:
    bucatini with cherry tomatoes and, 66
    in chopped Greek salad, 56
    in pan bagnat, 45
onions:
    caramelized, and bacon tart, 171
    rigatoni with squash and caramelized, 166–67
    in summer vegetable tian, 153
    white pearl, in boeuf bourguignon, 196
orange scallops on black rice, 113
    see also blood oranges

paella for a party, 87–88
pan bagnat, 45
pancetta:
    in rigatoni with squash and caramelized onions, 166–67
    chicken with lemon fries, 134–35
pan con tomate, 94
pappardelle with osso buco ragù, 206
paprika, smoked (pimentón), 89, 132
paprika roast chicken with root vegetables, 132–33
parchment paper, 14
    mushrooms baked in, 164
Parmigiano-Reggiano cheese:
    about, 55
    in rigatoni with squash and caramelized onions, 166–67
    in fennel and apple salad, 55
    in gnocchi topping for Italian shepherd's pie, 168–69
    in pistou (pesto), 182
    in polenta with caramelized corn, 83

in ricotta meatballs with tomato sauce, 76–77
in risotto cakes, 84
in semolina garlic bread, 98
in summer vegetable tian, 153
using leftover rinds of, 188
parsnips, in paprika roast chicken with root vegetables, 132–33
pasta:
    bucatini with cherry tomatoes and olives, 66
    pappardelle with osso buco ragù, 206
    peanut noodles with mango, 47
    rigatoni with squash and caramelized onions, 166–67
    whole-wheat penne with Swiss chard and walnuts, 69
pastry blender, 15
Pavlovas with strawberries and cream, 232–33
peach(es):
    in grilled stone fruit, 235
    Melba, 247
    pork chops with rosemary and grilled, 104–7
peanut dressing, for peanut noodles with mango, 47
pear(s):
    roasted, salad with Gorgonzola, 124
    roasted, with red wine, 248
    in winter fruit crisp, 242–43
peas, green:
    in paella for a party, 87–88
    puree, 189
    in soupe au pistou, 182
peas, sugar snap, in peanut noodles with mango, 47
pecans:
    in chocolate-chocolate chip cookies, 217
    in Sunday chicken with couscous stuffing, 129–31
peppers:
    in chunky gazpacho with avocado, 51
    piquillo, in paella for a party, 87–88
    roasted, 23
pistou (pesto), 182
pizza:
    dough, basic, 154, 155
    mushroom and Taleggio, 159
    radicchio and prosciutto, 155
    tomato and mozzarella, 158